D.

jul

# jul
## SWEDISH AMERICAN HOLIDAY TRADITIONS

*patrice m. johnson*

**MINNESOTA HISTORICAL SOCIETY PRESS**

The publication of this book was supported though a generous grant from the Dale S. and Elizabeth D. Hanson Fund for Swedish American History.

www.mnhspress.org

The Minnesota Historical Society Press is a member of the Association of American University Presses.

Manufactured in Canada

10 9 8 7 6 5 4 3 2 1

∞ The paper used in this publication meets the minimum requirements of the American National Standard for Information Sciences—Permanence for Printed Library Materials, ANSI Z39.48–1984.

International Standard Book Number

ISBN: 978-1-68134-043-2 (hardcover)

Library of Congress Cataloging-in-Publication Data available upon request.

Photos pages viii, 13, 35, 65 from pexels.com.

Photos pages 43, 60, 74, 138, 144, 161, 169, 175, 176, 190, 218, 223, 248 by Susan Everson, Anne Levin, and Shannon Pennefeather.

All other photographs by the author.

For my two role models,
Ted and Stephanie,

and to those departed
voices that continue
to call us to supper,

especially Grandpa Al,
who taught us dirty
Swedish limericks

# Swedish Meal Prayer

*I Jesu namn till bords vi gå,*
*Välsigna, Gud, den mat vi få,*
*Och hägna med din milda hand*
*I nåd vårt hem och fosterland.*

In Jesus's name to table we go
God bless the food we receive
And enclose with your gentle hand
The grace of our home and native land.

*jul*

# I hear the crackling

of tiny meatballs frying in butter, and the house is filled with a familiar heady perfume of beef, pork, and allspice. There is a nuance to the sound and smell, and I instinctively know when to turn the balls or remove them from the heat and add another dozen to the pan. If the smoke alarm goes off, I'll know I've channeled my late father, who was a notorious meatball burner.

Anyone who has ever made multiple batches of Swedish meatballs in a single afternoon knows that you lose count at fifty and the balls get bigger as the afternoon becomes evening. There is comfort in knowing that for more than one hundred years someone in my family has spent Christmas Eve standing watch over the meatballs.

For generations before me and generations to follow, the traditional dishes placed upon our *julbord* (Christmas table) honor our collective past, nourish our present, and demonstrate hope for our future. Food is a compelling tool for telling our stories, especially our stories of immigration. For immigrant families like mine, the simple but significant meatball is loaded with meaning.

My family pulled out our Swedish traditions mostly during the holidays. Our house was a good mash-up of Swedish and American celebration, and our post-Thanksgiving lead-up to Christmas was filled with Saturday afternoons painting the sugar cookies that mom baked and sprinkling rosettes with powdered sugar. I was beyond excited with each year's Christmas tree, so large that it practically pushed us out of our living room. All twelve months of my kid calendar rotated around annual viewings of *A Charlie Brown Christmas* and *Rudolph the Red-Nosed Reindeer*. When it was time to hang our stockings, we five sisters carefully patched up our names with a swath of glue and glitter, then hung the stockings in chronological order (mine being the smallest and last due to my position as the youngest). It was all so thrilling I could hardly bear it.

Yet the true thrill of it all was anticipating Christmas Eve dinner, when we would sit together at a table bursting with all manner of Swedish concoctions. Always present were typical Swedish *julbord* dishes like tiny allspice-kissed meatballs, boiled potatoes with "runny butter," fruit salad, and the borrowed Norwegian specialty lefse (served "Swedish style": warm with butter and never sugared). Before my time there was lutfisk, a cream sauce, dilled peas, and rice pudding. The meal also included a hefty hot dish of rather un-Swedish baked macaroni and cheese.

What makes this food Swedish? Is it dill, cream, or potatoes? Does it capture a time and place? Is it in the intention of those who bake the rye bread or roll tiny meatballs scented with allspice? Is it the Nordic way of contrasting yet balancing color and texture: pairing meat dishes with fruits, subdued whites and tans with bright berries and herbs? Is it the rich but not overly sweet desserts? Does this definition of Swedishness include the macaroni and cheese my family serves every Christmas Eve, just as our great-grandmother served it nearly one hundred years ago?

When I decided to pursue my master's degree in Swedish immigration and foodways, I began with an investigation into the roots of our macaroni and cheese entrée. I discovered a hidden narrative that illustrates how food traditions evolve when families blend. In 1932, Catholics did not eat meat on Christmas Eve. My mom suggested that the marriage between Lutheran Grandpa Elliot and Catholic Grandma Louise prompted Great-grandmother Johnson to add a meatless protein to the Christmas Eve menu. My great-grandmother placed a casserole of macaroni and cheese alongside the Swedish meatballs and lutfisk to make her daughter-in-law feel welcome.

However, Great-aunt Hazel recalled matters differently. "My mother made macaroni and cheese because it was Paul's favorite," she told me, referring to her older brother. Great-grandmother Johnson was Great-grandfather Johnson's second wife. She came to Minneapolis to care for three children who were left motherless when Great-grandfather's first wife died. She doted on all of her children, step- and biological, and none so much as handsome and charming Paul, who was especially appreciative of her cooking.

A classmate offered a third possible narrative to our macaroni and cheese tale. She suggested that my hot dish inheritance may be an example of early American food-ways adaptation, mentioning the southern, often black, tradition of macaroni and cheese both as a celebratory meal and as everyday fare. Macaroni and cheese is one of very few truly American dishes that cross regions.

I like the additional thread to our macaroni mystery. Now, I imagine that Great-grandmother Johnson served macaroni and cheese on Christmas Eve to welcome her Catholic daughter-in-law, and to make happy her favored son Paul, and to identify herself and her family as Americans.

As I researched my thesis, I encountered many other Minnesotans with Swedish ancestry who told me similar stories of family, food, and celebration. I also began to understand the custom of assimilation as it was practiced during the time when Swedes immigrated to our region. As with most American immigrants, Swedes experienced an assimilation process whereby they lost their costumes and language and began to *look* and *sound* like Americans. As they integrated into American society, they attended school and work with individuals from other ethnic groups, possibly marrying outside of their own group (as my grandma did). At this point, individuals act like Americans. A fully integrated individual *thinks* like an American, and ethnic traditions become celebrations of the past rather than of the present or in anticipation of the future. New traditions are created that emphasize evolving connections and identities.

This assimilation process explains how traditional immigrant foods were relegated to weekend meals and holiday tables, and possibly how macaroni and cheese came to appear at my family's *julbord*. If we are rooted in our host society, we eat food that is accepted by our neighbors. When we look to the future we explore some-times unfamiliar cuisines.

Ethnic foods can represent an idealized past. We are most nostalgic during the holidays, and those are the times when ethnic foods appear on our tables. The Swedish recipes that were set aside for weekend and holiday tables become the dishes that are especially cherished.

More than 1.5 million Swedes migrated to the United States in the 1800s through 1930. The majority of those Swedes settled in the Upper Midwest. Initially, the most common category of Swedish immigrants included families and sometimes entire folk communities attracted to abundant, inexpensive farmland. Rural immigrants without the means to purchase land settled in urban areas, spreading into the Dakotas, Nebraska, and Kansas. In larger cities such as Chicago and the Twin Cities, Swedes established themselves as a labor force, especially in mills and breweries. Single Swedish women were prized for their domestic abilities as au pairs, house-keepers, and cooks.

Before the turn of the nineteenth century, starvation, economic desperation, and religious oppression throughout Sweden triggered increasing numbers of young, single Swedish migrants to move to large cities, especially in Illinois, Iowa, and Minnesota. By 1900 Minnesota claimed the largest Swedish-born population in the nation, and an increase in labor opportunities drew nearly half of that population to Minneapolis and St. Paul.

Swedish emigrants to America brought with them two food genres: *husmanskost* (daily) and holiday food traditions. Both can still be seen in American recipes, old and new, in foods presented as Swedish. Interestingly, there is crossover in both Sweden and America as many traditionally *husmanskost* dishes, such as meatballs and pickled herring, are now served as part of a holiday menu.

*Husmanskost*—"house man's diet," or everyday food—developed out of the region and climate of Sweden. Freshwater fish and saltwater seafood form a cornerstone of Swedish cuisine as the land is surrounded by seas and filled with lakes, ponds, and rivers. In fact, kitchen middens containing herring bones date back to Neolithic times. For generations, northern Sami have raised reindeer for meat. Game such as venison, bear, rabbit, pheasant, and quail inhabit the forests and mountains. Mushrooms and lingonberries, cloudberries, and strawberries grow wild. In a climate that produces long, cold winters and brief summers, it was historically necessary to preserve foods in various forms: dried, salted, smoked, brined, and pickled. Root vegetables became an important part of a winter diet: parsnips, beets, rutabaga, and, more recently, potatoes.

Today we associate many foods and ingredients with Swedish cuisine: meatballs, rye bread, potatoes, cucumbers, salmon, Christmas cookies, wedding and apple cake, ham, pancakes, pea soup, aquavit, pork and cabbage, berries, meat with fruit, flat- and crispbreads, and coffee (especially as part of *fika*, the daily social event of sharing coffee and baked goods with coworkers, friends, and relatives). The herbs and

## ethnicity and foodways

spices of Swedish cuisine are clean and aromatic: dill, cardamom, caraway, anise, and fennel.

*Husmanskost*'s reach extends beyond foodways. Northern and midwestern regional characteristics and climate are similar to those in Sweden, and immigrants from Sweden often selected settlements based on that familiarity. Our region's landscape—with its abundance of dairy and farmland; lakes, rivers, and streams rich with fish; and forests and grasslands filled with wild berries and game—determined, in part, Swedish immigrants' choice of habitat. When Scandinavian ingredients such as rye, herring, and stout and barley beer were not available in northern America, Scandinavian immigrants sought out acceptable substitutes for the ingredients they missed.

Swedish American *jul* in the northern heartland is a celebration of our past, present, and future. Traditional Swedish cuisine typifies a family celebration: centerpiece holiday meals originating from immigrant ancestors' recipes. Our traditions honor those who came before us and link us to family and community, and they tell our collective story. Inspired by the hidden narrative to my family's macaroni and cheese hot dish, I began researching this book determined to learn about the holiday food and stories of fellow Swedish Americans who live in my region: amazing tales of immigration, reflections of a Swedish past, and celebration of the North American Midwest.

As I set to work on this project, I was struck by the number of people who informed me that what we consider to be Swedish cuisine in America is very different from what is considered to be Swedish cuisine in Sweden. In Sweden, national cuisine is continually evolving according to current events, exploration, and trends (just as American cuisine continually morphs into

**A note about the use of the complicated term *ethnic*.** "Ethnic" is often defined as coming from a heritage *outside* the mainstream population. In folklore theory, particularly, it has been developed to discuss foodways or cuisines that reflect 1) common heritage, 2) a heritage within a larger host culture (Chinese food would not be ethnic in China, for example), and 3) perception of distinctive heritage. Ethnic foods reflect all three of these characteristics, plus they are negotiations with the specific host community, so that the resulting foods reflect the tastes and ethos of that community as well.

Ethnicity in America summons controversies about what defines a "real American," although in the past passage into American citizenry was often marked by loss of ethnic identity. I use the term *ethnicity* here not to be inflammatory, but as a definition of original place. America is a country with a diverse population consisting of multiple ethnicities. When we consider our neighbor to be "The Ethnic Other," does doing so produce division or does it encourage a diverse and robust society?

a fusion of immigrant influence, nutritional and political beliefs, and other trends), although important characteristics that define Swedish foodways are retained. I tried to explain that this was the point of my research.

All foodways are influenced by place and time. Food is a dynamic phenomenon. Yet, much of the Swedish food we place on our celebratory tables is what our grandparents brought with them from a time long past. Certainly, the recipes, ingredients, and cooking techniques have evolved, yet the core of the dishes remains intact. The result is a unique regional Swedish American cuisine.

June through August 2016 became the Summer of *Jul* for my husband and me. We took day-trips to see important Swedish locales and interview willing participants. Most people I spoke with reported that during the holidays they eat a variety of Nordic foods, not just those deemed Swedish. Lefse, the delicate Norwegian potato bread, is especially popular (and not just at Christmas), as is the Christmas fruit bread *julkaka*. In Alexandria, Minnesota, I chatted with several people who told me they no longer differentiate between Swedes and Norwegians: "We're all the same, anyway."

Everywhere I went, I was often handed a well-worn copy of *Scandinavian Recipes* by Julia Peterson Tufford. A quick bookshelf scan demonstrated that I already owned three copies. Why did this book keep appearing in the storyline, and what did it want me to know? Why does a Norwegian American woman continue to wield such influence upon a huge portion of Scandinavian Americans and Canadians seventy-five years after the first printing of her cookbook?

The small paperback cookbook had dozens of printings, and I've seen it referenced by home cooks as far north as Canada, as far south as Missouri, east to Michigan, and west to Portland and Seattle. The first copyright date for *Scandinavian Recipes* is 1940, and I've seen editions dated as recent as 1973: an amazing example of successful self-publishing. This little book gets around, and yet relatively nothing is known about Julia Peterson Tufford.

Research often starts at an ending and works backward to find information about the beginning. I contacted historian Debbie Miller, who found Tufford's death certificate. Minneapolis *Star Tribune* "Taste" editor Lee Svitak Dean sent me an obituary. Google searches led me to churches and a printer, and eventually I found Tufford's son, Bob. I emailed him, and his response revealed the story of a beloved woman:

My mother was born in 1898. Her parents both came from Norway and met in Minneapolis. They homesteaded on a farm near Bagley where my mother was raised. I never met my grandfather but my grandmother lived with us for much of my youth. My mother graduated from Deaconess Hospital in Minneapolis around 1920 and did graduate work in Chicago. She became the head nurse in Pediatrics at Minneapolis General Hospital and was a career nurse until her marriage to my father in 1938. I was born in 1941 and the cookbook was in my life from my earliest memory.

I think that my mother collected recipes from her mother and other original sources. Once she became a mother she never worked outside the home and probably after being a career nurse she was needing some creative outlet. I am not sure how they initially developed a market for the book, but by the late forties it was actively being sold. My parents had the book printed and distributed it themselves through churches, ladies' aids, bookstores and somehow to a lot of individuals. I remember it was a big deal to get the mail because there were always orders every day from all over the U.S. and Canada.

My dad would wrap the books and mail them. He arranged for the book's printing for a long time with the Wadena paper (he had owned a small-town

"A simple r
A door that
friendlines
Father's ar d
ing faith-
Our pricele s
A kettle si
fire,
The fragrai u
freshly r
That was h

It is my pleasure to present to you th
edition of "Scandinavian Recipes", hoping
you pleasant memories of a dish "just lik:
ake.
The purpose of this book is to gather into
imple "folk recipes" that were so familiar i
ul mine, thus preserving them for the futu
folk songs they have a distinctive qualit:
No attempt is made in this booklet to
oking — my only wish is to share with
ection of Scandinavian recipes, whi
the red from many sources over a p

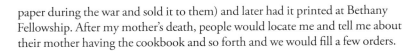

paper during the war and sold it to them) and later had it printed at Bethany Fellowship. After my mother's death, people would locate me and tell me about their mother having the cookbook and so forth and we would fill a few orders.

Eventually Bob sold the book rights to the distributor, and it remains in circulation nearly eighty years after the first printing. Bob says, "It was a big part of my heritage and a big deal in our home, often a needed part of my parents' income."

When I told him that *Scandinavian Recipes* reappears often in my research, Bob said, "I like that the book keeps popping up. Somehow its simplicity seems to make people remember it." He added, "I love that picture of my mother and the message she wrote in the beginning that shows her distinctive handwriting."

I asked Bob and his cousin Carolyn Engquist about the Christmas traditions in their family. Bob responded, "We mostly did Christmas at our home with some or all of my mother's five sisters and families at our place. My grandmother lived with us so that was part of the reason, as well as the fact my mother was the oldest and was known as a fine cook. My mother and grandmother would cook lefse and my mother would make various Christmas cookies. They also did of course lutefisk and *rommegrot* [cream pudding]. They would also have *julekage* and sometimes kringle. Meatballs would also be an option for us non-lutefisk people." Carolyn recalled,

> Long tables would be set up if the whole family was there, as there were six sisters, one brother, and a gaggle of cousins. The starter for the meal would be a small cup of *rommegrot*, topped with melted butter, cinnamon, and sugar. The main course could be turkey with all the trimmings, and there would always be lutefisk with drawn butter. The breads always included delicious, paper-thin potato lefse, and often rye bread. Dessert would probably include a wealth of Scandinavian pastries and cookies—deep fried rosettes and *fattigman* with powdered sugar, *sandbakkels*, spritz, rolled *krumkake*, sugar and ginger cookies cut in holiday shapes.

*Scandinavian Recipes* includes a detailed description and floor plan for *smörgåsbord*. I asked Carolyn if the description came from travel to Sweden. "I don't believe Julia had ever travelled to Scandinavia, and I assume her layout of the smorgasbord came from her association with Scandinavian groups and friends in the Twin Cities."

Carolyn continued, "Julia was my godmother, and I remember her kindness and gentleness as she taught us life's lessons. Her warmth and hospitality created so many happy occasions in our lives, and like her immediate family, I still miss her very much."

Writing this book and gathering the stories, recipes, and photos within it has been an honor. My quest meant testing a few hundred recipes, purchasing more pounds of butter and flour than I could count, road trips across the region to visit a Swedish language camp, a lutfisk producer, churches, historical societies, museums, and one very large statue of a Viking named Ole. Along the way I met and spoke to lovely, generous Swedish Americans willing to share their stories and recipes so that we can record the unique lore and cuisine of our region. I also looked at my mom with new gratitude, realizing that although she wasn't raised with Swedish traditions, she understood the importance of giving her daughters a foundation and appreciation of our heritage. My laptop screen is smeared with frosting from a test batch of ginger cookies, or maybe it was sugar, a reminder of the flavors I explored. Our dining room table became an office, stacked with a whiteboard to organize chapters and folders full of recipes and permissions. Eventually the papers were replaced with food props as our house became a recipe test kitchen and photo shoot locale. My coworkers generously consumed thousands of cookies, breads, rice puddings, and sausages on "reject Mondays," when I brought in food that wasn't camera ready.

Throughout the process, the politics of immigration surfaced not only in the stories I heard but in current events and a bruising political season across our country. While my people immigrated to America one hundred years ago or more, new immigrants continue to make their way to our borders. Immigration is never easy: leaving behind homes, family, friends, and everything familiar; perhaps fleeing war and unimaginable tragedies; losing identities. Destinies are usually a place unknown, and often come with unwelcoming neighbors.

Cultural differences have always divided us, until we learn that we have more in common with one another and have fewer disparities than we imagine—and that our diversity makes us stronger. I wonder why this lesson is so challenging for Americans to embrace. Our differences are cosmetic: skin color, costume, language, religion, and even the smells and flavors coming out of our kitchens. When we are invited to dine at a stranger's table, we begin to understand who they are and where they came from. Food tells our stories. Eating is a most intimate of acts, and eating together can alter our relationships. We sit down as strangers; we rise in our acceptance of one another.

# recipe notes

Unless otherwise noted, **eggs** used in these recipes are large.

**Fresh herbs and spices** are preferred. Buy whole nutmeg, allspice, and cardamom pods. Use a zester to grate nutmeg, a coffee or spice grinder to grind allspice, and a mortar and pestle to remove cardamom from its pods and then smash. If your retailer offers a variety of cardamom, reach for the green pods as they are most common in Swedish baking.

In recipes calling for **milk**, use whole milk unless otherwise noted. Use of scalded milk in recipes is an old practice dating back to a time before milk was pasteurized. The scalding destroyed dangerous bacteria as well as an enzyme that prohibited thickening. The use of warm milk (no hotter than 110 degrees) also aids in yeast rising. If you scald your milk, be sure to cool it down before adding yeast.

Many older recipes call for **margarine** or **vegetable shortening** rather than **butter**. Many recipes also call for lard. In some situations, ingredient availability or health beliefs dictated which fat was used. Vegetable shortening and lard have a lower water content than butter does, and the use of these fats produces flakier baked goods. However, butter has more flavor. Butter also melts faster than its fatty coun-

terparts, producing cookies that spread versus those that rise. In these instances, use the fat that produces the cookies you prefer. For cookie recipes that call for butter, allow butter to stand at room temperature for thirty minutes before blending or adding to a recipe. Butter is always unsalted unless otherwise noted.

**Yeast breads** have their own personalities, and they vary according to the temperature and humidity that surrounds them. If a recipe tells you the bread will double in an hour but your loaf is not complying, relax and let the bread do its thing on its own time.

None of these recipes specify dark versus light **molasses** and **brown sugar**. Follow your own taste. If you prefer a robust flavor, reach for dark.

**Vanilla sugar** is common in modern Swedish baking. If you have a Scandinavian specialty store, ask for it. Or order online. For a substitute, slice a vanilla bean in half lengthwise and add it to two or three pounds of sugar. Sugar will be fragrant within a few hours, but leave at least overnight for best results. Whisk sugar before using to break up any moisture clumps and to disperse vanilla. This same technique can be used with confectioner's sugar.

*Pepparkakor* (page 63)

*one*

ADVENT:
DARKNESS
& LIGHT

# Out of the darkness

of winter comes St. Lucia to light our way and Thursday night pea soup to warm our tummies.

The Swedish holiday food calendar begins with Advent, often including the tradition of Thursday night *ärtsoppa* (yellow pea soup) and *plättar* (small Swedish pancakes, ideally cooked in a pan with small round divots that shape the cakes). *Plättar* are a common dessert, while *pannkakor*, larger crêpe-like cakes, are more typically on the breakfast table. Dessert *plättar* are served with lingonberries and cream, and while maple syrup is not common in Nordic countries, it is used rather prolifically across America's Upper Midwest, including in our desserts.

The *ärtsoppa* tradition dates back to a century during which Catholic rule came to Sweden and meat was forbidden on Fridays as well as Thursday evenings. The soup is said to have been used to assassinate King Erik XIV, who consumed a bowl laced with arsenic in the late 1500s. Although fashionable for centuries, Sweden's national dish is a Thursday-night custom losing popularity with younger generations. Now, rather than being a vegetarian staple, *ärtsoppa* is typically served over or alongside pork, whether ham, loin, or roasted. Pair with beer, aquavit, and *punsch*.

I first read about *ärtsoppa* in my trusty Time-Life Foods of the World series volume *The Cooking of Scandinavia & Recipes: The Cooking of Scandinavia*. This book by Dale Brown opened my eyes to life as a Swede beyond Minneapolis and made me curious about how the food traditions in Sweden differed from those I grew up with. I'd already spent a few years abroad, including some formative years in Japan, where I explored their foodways with far too much caution.

Back in America I was ready to continue exploring, but with a more comfortable and familiar starting place. Yellow Pea Soup looked similar to Mom's split pea, although the color was different. A few lumps of pink ham floated alongside diced carrot and other less obvious vegetables. What intrigued me, besides the promise of an inexpensive but robust winter meal, was that the *Cooking of Scandinavia* recipe for *Ärter med flask* (pea soup with pork) instructs cooks to poke an onion with whole cloves and add it to the soup as it simmers. The clove-poked onion provides a delicate yet complicated flavor. What a novel idea! Although at the time I didn't know how to pronounce it, *ärtsoppa* and its festive companion Swedish pancakes worked their way into our weekly menu—and my heart.

First imported to Sweden by the Swedish East India Company in 1733, Swedish *punsch* is the preferred beverage for Thursday-night soup. The dark liqueur is thick and sweet, with (at least to my untrained palate) leather-meets-vanilla coffee notes reminiscent of Kahlúa, rounded out with a whiff of allspice, molasses, and cloves. Inhale deeper and you may detect a hint of licorice, caramel, and orange. *Punsch* is made from arrack (a distilled alcohol of fermented sap of coconut flowers, sugarcane, grain, or fruit) combined with rum or brandy and spices. A variety of imported commercial *punsch* is available in specialty liquor stores, especially during the holidays. Traditionally, *punsch* is served warm.

# Swedish **Pea Soup**

Adapted from a recipe provided by Faye Olson, Brooklyn Park, Minnesota

"This recipe was used in the old Coffee Stuga [at the American Swedish Institute in Minneapolis, Minnesota] on Wednesday evenings for the soup and sandwich suppers."

1 pound yellow peas (about 2 cups)

1–2 smoked ham hocks

2 teaspoons vegetable oil

1 large yellow or white onion, chopped fine

2 carrots, chopped fine

2 stalks celery, chopped fine

½ teaspoon dried thyme

salt and pepper

Soak peas in 4 cups cold water overnight.

Score fat on ham hock(s) and place in heavy saucepan. Cover with water and boil 1 to 2 hours or until meat begins to fall apart. Remove hock(s) from broth. Skim fat from broth and set aside about 4 cups of broth.

Remove meat from cooled hock(s), picking and pulling as much as you can from bone; there will not be much meat. Dice meat and reserve in broth; discard bone.

Place peas and soaking water in large stockpot and bring to simmer. Cook peas until just tender; about 45 to 60 minutes for split peas, 90 minutes for whole.

Add vegetable oil to skillet set over medium heat and add onions, carrots, and celery. Cook, stirring, until tender, about 5 minutes. Add vegetables, ham, broth, and thyme to peas. Simmer until thick, about 30 minutes. Season to taste with salt and pepper. Freezes well.

**MAKES ABOUT 20 CUPS (5 QUARTS)**

# Konung Gustaf's *Bästa Soppa*

Pea soup from the *Priscilla Art Cook Book*, published in 1948
by First Lutheran Church in Kansas City, Missouri

2 cups yellow peas

6 cups cold water (see tip)

1 pound pork (fresh or slightly cured)

2 teaspoons salt

¼ teaspoon ground ginger

Rinse peas and soak overnight. Drain and place in a large stockpot with enough cold water to cover the peas by an inch; let it come to a boil slowly, then cook vigorously for about 1 hour to make the skins come off more easily. As skins float to the surface, skim them off. When peas have cooked 1 hour, add pork and simmer about 2 hours, adding water as it simmers off so that peas are always covered by about an inch. Add seasonings. Cut pork into serving pieces. Serve in the soup or separately.

**SERVES 10**

 **TIP:** ¼ teaspoon baking soda may be added to water if water is hard.

# Rum *Punsch*

1 ½ ounces dark rum

¾ ounce Swedish *punsch*

¾ ounce freshly squeezed orange juice

Pour all ingredients into shaker with lots of ice. Shake, then strain into cocktail glass filled with ice. Float orange slice on top for garnish.

**SERVES 1**

# Updated *Ärtsoppa*
## (Yellow Pea Coconut Curry)

As with many of my personal recipes, I've updated the flavors of traditional *ärtsoppa* with ingredients borrowed from other lands. This version of yellow pea soup includes crispy fried Norwegian potato bread (lefse), coconut milk, yogurt, jalapeños, lime, and cilantro. The marriage brings new life to an old soup.

2 tablespoons vegetable oil

1 red onion, chopped (about ¾ cup)

3 cloves garlic, smashed

2 tablespoons grated fresh ginger

2–3 tablespoons prepared Thai red curry paste

1 teaspoon salt

1 teaspoon pepper

3 carrots, chopped

1 large russet or Yukon potato, chopped

1 pound (2 cups) yellow peas, soaked in cold water overnight and drained

8 cups low-sodium chicken or vegetable broth

1 (15-ounce) can coconut milk

2 tablespoons freshly squeezed orange juice (about ½ orange)

garnishes (see below)

Add oil to large stockpot on medium-high heat; add onions and cook, stirring, until translucent, about 5 minutes. Stir in garlic, ginger, and curry paste and cook an additional 30 to 60 seconds. Add salt, pepper, carrots, potato, peas, and broth. Increase heat if necessary to bring soup to a simmer; cover and cook until peas are tender, about 45 to 60 minutes for split peas, 90 minutes for whole. Check soup occasionally and stir, adding a few cups of water if soup becomes too thick.

Use an immersion blender or food processor to carefully puree the hot soup. Return to heat and stir in coconut milk and orange juice. Heat thoroughly. Garnish with cilantro-lime yogurt, lingonberry preserves, jalapeño slices, and crisped lefse strips. Serve with hot sauce on the side.

### For garnish

8 ounces unflavored Greek yogurt
2 tablespoons minced cilantro, plus more for topping
zest of ½ lime plus 1 tablespoon lime juice
pinch cumin
Whisk together yogurt, cilantro, lime zest and juice, and cumin.

vegetable oil
2 (8-inch) lefse rounds, cut into thin strips
Add enough vegetable oil to a large, heavy stockpot or Dutch oven to reach 1 inch; heat vegetable oil to 350 to 375 degrees. Deep-fry lefse strips for 1 to 2 minutes; drain on paper towels. (Alternatively: coat lefse strips with nonstick spray and bake at 350 degrees for about 10 minutes, turning once.)

1–2 jalapeños, sliced thin
lingonberry preserves

**SERVES 6–8**

Updated Ärtsoppa

Cindy Ostberg contacted me about a cookbook she owned, published in 1934 by my late great-great-uncle's parish, the Swedish Tabernacle Church in Minneapolis (formerly located at Tenth Avenue South and South Seventh Street, across the street from the Swedish Hospital, aka Hennepin County Medical Center nurse dormitories).

We met in her south Minneapolis home, where we pored over her family treasures, including many of her mother's cooking tools and the church cook-book. "My mother's markings are in there. She always said that was her bible for cooking."

One of the kitchen tools on Cindy's table was a cast-iron *plättar* griddle, with its individual wells that form batter into small pancakes. Cindy's grandfather made the griddles during his years at the Moline Foundry in Minneapolis. Both her father and grandfather worked in the foundry. "Grandpa Karl made these for gifts. I found this out because at reunions people would say, 'We have one of those!'"

Cindy opened the cookbook and said, "There is something in here I was looking at this morning. It is a pancake recipe, and it really brought up some mem-ories. My dad was the one that always made Swedish pancakes." She found a recipe cut from a newspaper taped to the cookbook page. "This is the recipe my dad used. This is the one."

"One time my father was robbed at the liquor store where he worked and the man took his wallet. My dad just kept saying to the police officer, 'Please try to find my wallet! I don't care about my license; I don't care about the money. I had a very special Swedish pancake recipe.' It was months later that the police officers did find the wallet. There wasn't any identification in it, but the police officer remem-bered that my father said there was a Swedish pan-cake recipe in there." The wallet and recipe were returned to Cindy's dad.

*Plättar*

**This recipe makes a very thin pancake. I beat the eggs until they are thick and lemon colored, and add an additional ¼ to ½ cup flour to the recipe. Use a *plättar* pan if you have one; otherwise, carefully form round cakes using 1 ½ to 2 tablespoons of batter for each 3-inch cake.**

*Cindy's dad's Swedish pancakes recipe*
*as written in the newspaper*

Serves 4

| | |
|---|---|
| 3 eggs | 1 tablespoon sugar |
| 1 ½ cups milk | ¾ cup flour, unsifted |
| ½ teaspoon salt | ½ teaspoon baking powder |
| 3 tablespoons melted butter or oil | |

Beat eggs. Add half the milk and dry ingredients and beat. Add remaining milk.

"I always used the special Swedish pancake frypan with seven sections. The cook better not plan to eat until the family is finished, as after the seventh section is poured, the first is ready to turn. Takes a big tablespoonful of the thin mixture for each section. It's my best way of getting eggs down the kids."

*Mrs. Herbert E. Bloomquist*

Pointing to the recipe she said, "This is the recipe. This paper was in the wallet . . . it was so special that Mom taped it into the cookbook." We continued reading the recipe and puzzling as to why this particular clipping was so important to Cindy's dad. "And why he carried it around. Why in his wallet?" We both wondered why he didn't memorize the recipe, and what possessed him to start making pancakes in the first place.

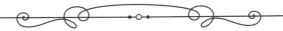

I wasn't sure what to expect when speaking with former Minnesota governor Arne Carlson. What I got was an enthusiastic man who peppered our conversation with interjections of "Marvelous!" and "Spectacular."

Carlson grew up in New York City. "We were poor, but everyone was poor. I remember that during World War II, in spite of the fact that we were poor, my parents always sent back food care packages to [their families in] Sweden." Christmases in the Bronx, he told me, "were quite spectacular!" He eagerly began listing the foods that appeared on the *jul* table. "We always had Swedish *sill*; Swedish caviar—herring roe; hardtack, the round kind with the hole in the center. There was always a ham. Meatballs are without question the best."

"[My parents] had lutfisk, clearly the most awful dish invented by man. But they did not insist that my brothers and I eat it." Once Carlson's mother over-cooked the lutfisk, and all these decades later he continues to chuckle at the occurrence. "Mom melted it into jelly. I thought that was a glorious event."

Carlson's parents were both Swedish immigrants, and while they each had ties to the Midwest (his mother lived in Illinois for a time, and his father in Wisconsin and Michigan), eventually both wound up in New York. Carlson's father was a musician, and his trio played at a Swedish gathering where he met Carlson's mother. They married, and while raising their three sons they spoke Swedish to one another. "But to us they spoke English. They were sensitive to us growing up with knowledge of American culture." During Christmas the family always sang carols, "some sung in English, some in Swedish, some a mixture of the two. There was always a great deal of fun."

During the holidays, "we always had a wonderfully decorated Christmas tree. We got the tree early, and it was always big. We'd spend days decorating it. Then we kept it up until March 4." Carlson explained,

"Dad's birthday was March 3, and my parents just thought it was appropriate" to keep the tree up through his birthday.

Carlson recalled that every Christmas Eve Santa made a visit to his home. Just before Santa arrived, Carlson's father would go out to get milk. "I would beg him not to leave. He would miss Santa!" Santa would visit the house, dressed "in terrible costumes." Carlson paused and stated, "Children see what they want to believe."

Carlson asked if I'd ever seen the movie *A Christmas Story*. The movie is a nostalgic look back at Christmas in the early 1940s Midwest. "That movie in many, many ways paralleled us. We dreamed of BB guns, and they were advertised on the back page of comics. I always wanted a red wagon [Radio] Flyer, a sled, and a BB gun. Of course, they never received serious consideration," Carlson smiled at the memories, telling me that the high cost of those dream toys meant they'd never be his.

"The most amazing gift I ever received was when I was in school. After World War II somebody invented a ballpoint pen. It was about a foot long, maybe longer. I lusted after that. I thought that was the ultimate in human technology. And I got one! It cost a full ten cents. That was my big Christmas present. To this day that was my best present ever." Carlson paused at the memory. "Now we give too many presents."

Of modern holidays, Carlson says, "I always have hardtack in the house. To this day we always have meatballs—*köttbullar*, herring roe, except we don't have that awful lutfisk. Lutfisk should be rel-egated to Norway. There is no reason for smart Swedes to eat lutfisk."

Carlson recalled the Thanksgiving his family spent after a year in Sweden. It was like starting from scratch, with his father taking on building management and the family living in a basement apartment. "We were so poor, we couldn't afford Thanksgiving dinner. I don't know what we were eating that day, but it wasn't turkey." Meanwhile, the upstairs tenants were preparing their feasts. One woman put her turkey out on the fire escape, either to cool before dinner or perhaps because there was no space in her kitchen. "We heard a terrific sound, and my brothers and I ran outside to see what the noise was. And there on the ground was a whole cooked turkey!" Carlson told me they brought that turkey into their apartment and ate every bit of it. Laughing at the memory, Carlson wondered what their neighbor thought when she went down to retrieve her bird and it was gone. "Her turkey flew away!"

When asked for a favorite recipe, Arne Carlson replied, "The recipe I would pick is Swedish pancakes as described by my wife, Susan, in *Minnesota Times & Tastes: Recipes & Menus Seasoned with History from the Minnesota Governor's Residence*. Susan Carlson's original recipe appears with the caveat, "The Carlsons prefer these pancakes with light maple syrup." However, Carlson told me, "I personally prefer lingonberries."

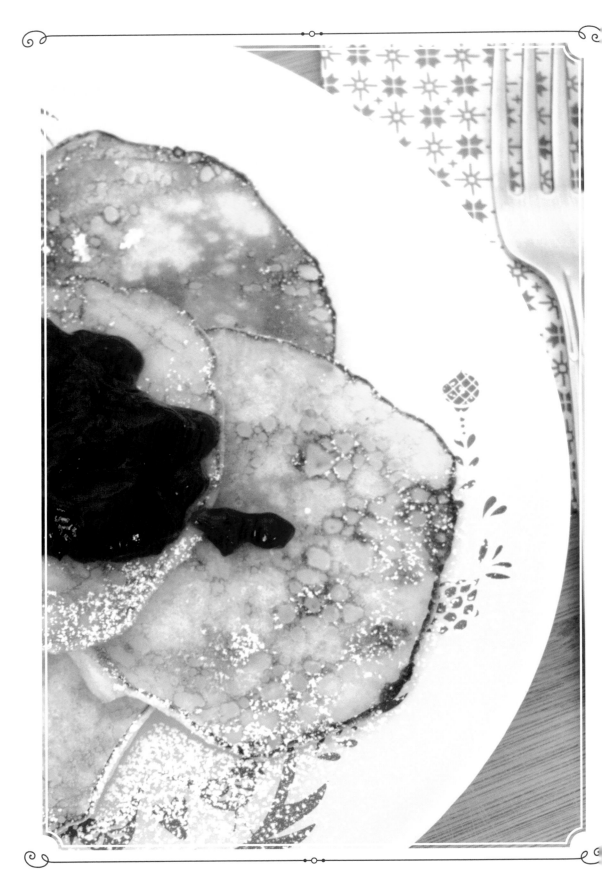

# Arne's **Swedish Pancakes**

Adapted from *Minnesota Times & Tastes*

½ cup flour

⅛ teaspoon salt

½ teaspoon baking powder

1 tablespoon sugar

2 eggs, beaten

1 cup milk

3 tablespoons butter, melted

1 teaspoon vanilla extract

In large mixing bowl, combine flour, salt, baking powder, and sugar. Add eggs; gradually beat in milk and melted butter. Stir in vanilla.

Pour 3-inch circles onto lightly greased hot skillet or griddle (or use *plättar* or silver dollar pancake griddle). When bubbles begin to form on top of cakes, flip and continuing cooking until both sides are golden brown.

Decorate tops with confectioner's sugar if desired. Serve with butter, maple syrup, and lingonberries.

**SERVES 4–6**

# Nordic ware

I met Dorothy Dalquist, her daughter Susan Dalquist Brust, and grand-daughter Jennifer Dalquist during the Scandinavian festival Norsk Høstfest in Minot, North Dakota. We were the Twin Cities contingent, guests of the festival and Nordic Kitchen headliners, performing cooking demos a few hours each day. Dorothy was an esteemed guest of honor, receiving induction into the Scandinavian-American Hall of Fame for lifetime achievements. As she passed through the halls on the first day of the festival, crowds parted to allow her through; she's practically a religious figure to those who appreciate Nordic Ware design and functionality.

Back in Minneapolis, I chatted with Dorothy and Susan, and listened to Dorothy's stories of strength and unwitting matriarchy. "I was named Dorothy because I was a gift from God," she told me. Dorothy's Danish parents had two grown daughters living in California when Dorothy was born, and she was only three years old when her mother died. She said, "I knew her through my sisters and through food." Her sisters and aunts helped keep the memory of Dorothy's mother alive as they shared beloved recipes.

Dorothy met Dave Dalquist in Chicago. She was nineteen years old, visiting the Art Institute, and he was a twenty-five-year-old engineer. Eventually he was hired at General Mills, where he worked in plas-

tics and moldings, and the couple settled in Minneapolis to raise their family. Dave and his brother invented a plastic that didn't melt when it came in contact with hot aluminum. In 1946 the brothers bought Northland Aluminum and began building an empire.

For the first three years of their marriage, Dorothy and Dave lived with his parents. Dorothy's mother-in-law, Mabel, liked to say she was "100 percent Swedish." She was a master in the kitchen, and her influence extended to her sons' business. It was Mabel who suggested the brothers try their hand at cookware, because she knew other Scandinavian Americans wanted access to the same baking and stovetop cookware that was available in Sweden, Denmark, and Norway. Soon, rosette and *krumkake* irons and *aebleskiver* griddles landed in kitchens where cooks sought to make authentic Nordic treats. In fact, the popularity of Nordic Ware's *plätte* (Swedish for flat) pancake pans helped coin the phrase that makes brunch chefs shiver: silver dollar pancakes.

American-made Nordic Ware is most famous for its Bundt cake pan, and its factory churns out dozens of new shapes and sizes every year. Nordic Ware continues to be family owned and operated and is still headquartered in Minnesota. The company now employs more than 350 people who produce hundreds of products—all directed by Dorothy's steadying hand.

St. Lucia is a glimpse into the coming holiday season. At dawn on December 13, Swedish families wake to the procession of St. Lucia, complete with songs and children dressed as the saint and her court.

Lucia, the martyred Saint of Light, provides light during the dark season. Saffron buns are the traditional breakfast served with hot coffee and other baked goods. Several accounts of Lucia exist, including:

> Lucia, a beautiful Sicilian virgin, sells her dowry and gives the money to the poor as gratitude to God for allowing her mother to recover from an illness. Her heathen fiancé sends her to the Roman prefect, and she is sentenced to work in a brothel. When the arresting officers come for her, she cannot be moved. She is stripped and encircled by fire, but remains unmoved and unharmed. Finally, the soldiers execute her with a sword.

> Lucia is a Christian virgin with beautiful eyes. Lucia gouges out her eyes and impresses a heathen prince who converts to Christianity, and God bequeaths Lucia with the reward of eyes even more beautiful than the first pair.

> Lucia delivers food to prisoners within the Roman catacombs. Her hands full of the gifts, she illuminates her path with a crown of lights.

How and why did Lucia become a Swedish icon? Is she a remnant of Catholic rule? Whatever the origins of Sweden's St. Lucia, she is a welcome symbol of light and salvation during one of the longest and darkest nights of the year. December 13 was once referred to as the night of the trolls. As with so many folk traditions that are replaced with Christian substitutes, Lucia and the trolls are now symbolically morphed. Lucia's association with the devil stems from that earlier belief, and many understood her to be the leader of the trolls. Her name being the female equivalent of Lucifer did not help her reputation.

It wasn't until the 1800s that Lucia became the saint of light and goodness, and it wasn't until 1927 that her holiday took off as a national celebration, when the Swedish newspaper *Stockholms-Tidningen* began an effort to increase Christmas shopping. Their marketing campaign popularized Lucia with processionals headed by a white-clad (symbolizing purity) and red-sashed (symbolizing martyrdom) Lucia, whose head is crowned with glowing candles (modern Lucia wears a battery-operated crown) to signify the light she brings.

Today, every Swedish home, school, community, and hospital hosts a Lucia event, sometimes with competitions among young girls vying to be selected as St. Lucia. December 13 dawns with St. Lucia processionals, complete with singing children dressed as Lucia and her court of white-dressed girls and cone-hatted, wand-wielding Star Boys, bearing gifts of golden buns.

You don't need to live in Sweden, dress in white, or don a crown of candles to partake in Lucia's Day. In America, modern Lucia processionals occur in museums and churches where Swedish traditions are honored. IKEA sells the buns, and many Scandinavian bakeries have added Lucia buns to their cases. But the best way to enjoy Lucia buns is by adding the tasty treat to your holiday baking repertoire.

St. Lucia saffron buns can be shaped in numerous forms. Lore dates the shapes, as well as the saffron, to ancient Mesopotamia. Most popular today is the S shape, often mistakenly called *lussekatt* (Lucia cat). The true identity of the popular shape is *julgalt*, or Christmas boar, perhaps in reference to a pig's curly tail. ✍

# St. Lucia Rolls

Gustavus Adolphus College, St. Peter, Minnesota

"Served during the Christmas holiday season as a sweet bread, St. Lucia Rolls are a signature on the luncheon buffet at the celebration of the Festival of St. Lucia."

1 packet (2 ¼ teaspoons) active dry yeast

¼ cup warm water

¼ cup milk, warmed

¼ cup sugar

¼ cup margarine, softened

1 egg

⅛ teaspoon salt

⅛ teaspoon cardamom, crushed

⅛ teaspoon orange zest

2 ¼ cups flour (about 18 ounces), divided

48 raisins

egg wash (1 egg whisked with 1 tablespoon water)

coarse sanding sugar

Dissolve yeast in warm water in bowl of stand mixer. Stir in milk, sugar, margarine, egg, salt, cardamom, orange zest, and half of the flour. Fit mixer with dough hook and knead dough until smooth. Alternatively, knead dough with a strong arm and a wooden spoon. Stir in enough of the remaining flour to make a dough that is easy to handle—soft but not sticky. Cover and let rise in a warm place for 45 minutes.

Preheat oven to 350 degrees and grease baking sheets or line with parchment paper. Punch down dough and divide into 24 balls, about 1 ounce each. Shape each ball into an 8-inch rope by rolling with hands on a floured surface. Curl both ends of rope in opposite directions to make a compact S-shaped, coiled roll. Place a raisin in the center of each coil and place rolls about 2 inches apart on prepared baking sheets. Lightly brush tops of rolls with egg wash and sprinkle with sanding sugar. Let rise in a warm place for 35 minutes. Bake rolls for 8 to 10 minutes, or until golden brown.

**MAKES ABOUT 24 ROLLS**

 **NOTE:** This recipe does not include the traditional saffron, but the cardamom and orange impart a distinct flavor.

Swedish Crown Bakery is partially hidden among the small shops of a strip mall in Anoka, Minnesota. I parked the car and followed my nose toward the ethereal scents of cardamom and rye yeast breads.

Inside the bakery, overstimulated by the choices, I boldly ordered a half dozen pastries, cookies, and one limpa (Swedish rye bread). Satisfied with my loot, I sat down with bakery owner Eva Sabet to talk about the holidays and her famous kringle.

Eva's parents migrated to Malmö, Sweden, from Hungary, and Eva's mother soon began working in a chocolate factory. While the sweet flavors of her childhood continue to influence Eva, she admits her baking business "all started with a kringle." When she arrived in America more than a decade ago, Eva worked at the small café in the basement of the American Swedish Institute (ASI). Eva was the only real Swedish baker in the community, and the woman who ran the café asked her to make a kringle. After some experimentation, Eva developed a recipe and technique that wowed customers and drew her into the bakery business.

During a successful stint baking at their local co-op, Eva and her husband Fari decided to concentrate their efforts at their own bakery while continuing to focus on healthful, organic, wholesome ingredients and offering delicious goodies for people with dietary issues.

A few months after our conversation, I busied myself in the teaching kitchen at ASI. The lights were dimmed, candles glowed, and a table overflowing with pastries awed the guests as they found their seats for the start of a Swedish holiday baking class. On the stove, rice was cooking for a pudding to be topped with lingonberry and raspberry sauce. Eva calmly plated a pile of *lussebullar* (saffron-scented Lucia buns), still warm after a car ride from Swedish Crown Bakery. She added the platter to the table next to a ribbon-wrapped gingerbread Bundt, chocolate-covered fruit, *pepparkakor*, *mandelmussla*, *klenäter*, and a huge bowl of tangerines. The guests gasped with appreciation at each new addition.

As class began, Eva wove together her health philosophy, cooking tips, and Swedish baking history. *"Pepparkakor* were first eaten as a medicine," she told the class. Imported from Germany (where they had been imported from Mesopotamia), ginger cookies appeared in Sweden in the early 1300s. Nearly a century later, nuns began baking the cookies to sell at markets and pharmacies. Touted for the healing properties in ginger, honey, potassium-rich potash, and spices, the cookies were eaten to maintain stomach health and heal tummy aches. "It was believed that *pepparkakor* made men nicer," Eva continued. Rigorous men only consumed meat and wine, but kind men enjoyed cookies, and the spices of a *pepparkake* were said to mellow out a harsh man.

Eva explained that in Sweden Christmas cookies don't get the kind of attention they do in America. Swedes prefer breads and chocolate-dipped fruits. "In Sweden, there are two hundred kinds of bread," Eva said. She described her most recent trip home and how she wanted to try every single loaf.

"If you could have any food, prepared by anyone living or dead, what Christmas treat would you choose?" I asked Eva. She smiled and answered quickly, *"Töltött kaposzta."* Of the Hungarian stuffed cabbage, Eva says, "That is the taste of Christmas." ⅃⅃

# *Lussebulle* (Lucia Buns)

Eva Sabet, Anoka, Minnesota

1 cup (2 sticks) salted butter

2 cups milk

1 cup Greek-style yogurt

¼–½ teaspoon ground
(or crushed; see tips) saffron

1 ¼ cups sugar, divided

2 teaspoons salt

7–8 cups flour

2 packets (4 ½ teaspoons) dry
yeast or 1.7 ounces fresh yeast

1 cup raisins, soaked in water or rum

egg wash (1 egg whisked with
1 tablespoon water)

In a small saucepan, melt the butter.
Remove from heat and add milk. Let cool to
room temperature. Stir in yogurt.

Soak the saffron in 1 tablespoon of the sugar
and 2 tablespoons hot water.

In a large mixing bowl, whisk together
remaining sugar, salt, and flour. Stir in buttermilk mixture, saffron mixture, yeast, and raisins
and knead for 10 minutes by hand or using a
stand mixer with dough hook. Place dough
in an oiled bowl, cover, and let stand until
doubled in size, about 1 ½ hours.

Now the shaping can begin! Divide dough
into about 20 equal portions. Play around
with the shape of the dough: twist one rope
into the popular S-shape or a pretzel; lay two
ropes together and twist the four ends away
from one another to look like a cat's whiskers;
twist one rope around another to look like
a swaddled baby; lay three ropes on top of
one another and twist them into a bread wig
of Lucia's hair. Put the buns on a parchment-
lined baking sheet, cover with a kitchen
towel, and set in a warm, draft-free area. Let
rise until buns are almost doubled in size,
about 45 minutes.

Preheat oven to 425 degrees. Brush buns with
egg wash for a nice shine. Bake until golden,
5 to 7 minutes, depending on size of buns.
Let cool. Brush with melted butter and dip in
sugar, if desired.

**MAKES ABOUT 20 ROLLS,
DEPENDING ON SIZE AND SHAPE**

**EVA'S BAKING TIPS:** Always use **salted** butter: it has more flavor.
Crushing saffron releases its flavor. Crush saffron threads before softening
in liquid and adding to recipes. To crush, add threads to a piece of paper,
fold paper in half, and use the non-blade end of a knife to press the paper
against the threads. (Or use a mortar and pestle to grind the threads.)

# Updated *Lussebullar*

This updated version swaps cranberries for raisins and includes seasonally abundant tangerines. I dissolve the saffron in a mix of aquavit and sugar, but you can substitute vodka, rum, brandy, or plain water for the aquavit.

ᴗ ᴗ

2 cups milk, heated to just under 110 degrees

1 teaspoon vanilla extract

1 packet (2 ¼ teaspoons) active dry yeast

½ cup sugar, divided

2 tablespoons aquavit (see head note)

1 teaspoon powdered saffron

zest plus juice of 2 tangerines

4 ½–5 ½ cups flour

1 teaspoon ground cardamom

1 teaspoon salt

24 whole dried cranberries

confectioner's sugar

Combine milk, vanilla, yeast, and a pinch of the sugar in a small bowl and let sit for 10 minutes. In another small bowl combine aquavit, 1 teaspoon of the sugar, saffron, and zest; stir until saffron dissolves.

In a large bowl, whisk together 4 cups flour, remaining sugar, cardamom, and salt. Make a well in the center and pour in the milk-yeast mixture and saffron mixture. Stir to form soft dough, gradually adding more flour as necessary. Turn the dough out onto a floured surface and knead until the dough is smooth and elastic, about 10 minutes. Shape the dough into a ball; place in large oiled bowl, turning to coat, and cover with plastic wrap or a kitchen towel. Let rise until doubled in size, about 2 hours.

Gently fold dough and divide into 12 equal pieces. Shape each piece into an S and place the rolls 2 inches apart on a greased baking sheet. Push whole cranberry into each crease of the "S." Cover with plastic wrap or a kitchen towel and let rise until almost doubled, about 1 hour.

Preheat oven to 375 degrees. Bake rolls for 30 minutes or until each roll sounds hollow when tapped. Cool on rack; stir together tangerine juice and confectioner's sugar to make a glaze. Brush buns with glaze.

**MAKES 12 LARGE ROLLS**

# two

## PREPARATION & BAKING

*Gen Xers, that cohort*
born after the Baby Boomers populated the world, share universal childhood memories of Christmas preparation. Our holiday season began with annual viewings of *A Charlie Brown Christmas* and *Rudolph the Red-Nosed Reindeer*, decorating the tree (whether aluminum, artificial, or pine), and helping (aka interfering) as the adults baked endless trays of cookies.

In our house, the cookies were off-limits until Christmas Eve. The cruelty of this situation was not lost on me. I played on the large, round rag rug underneath the enormous Christmas tree. Barbie and Skipper drove their camper beneath the glittering boughs, explorers in the redwood forest, while from the kitchen came the intoxicating aromas of baking: sugar, almond, vanilla, an occasional whiff of chocolate. The entire house was filled with smells of pine and cookies. It was more than I could bear.

There were endless shapes, sizes, flavors, and textures. Some were baked, others fried, and there was even a year with chocolate rum balls. So many cookies; so little permission to eat them all. Mom made each of us our favorite cookie and added something new and different to her selection every year.

One weekend afternoon each season was reserved for decorating the sugar cookies. It was the only time we girls were allowed in the kitchen to do anything more than set the table or wash dishes, and it was magical. We sat down with paintbrushes and bowls of brightly colored frosting as mom placed a platter of cookies in front of us. We tried to be clever, creating green Santas and blue trees. To my young eyes, every cookie was beautiful.

Mom packed the cookies neatly into Tupperware, enamel pots, and every available container. She stored the cookies on the porch, where the cold weather made for freezer-like conditions. Each container had a unique form and color, and she always put the same style of cookie into a particular crock. This was how my sisters and I knew where to find our favorite cookies.

My sisters were amazing at stealing cookies, and they taught me the art of sneaking cookies without getting caught. They were masters at restacking cookies and filling in empty spaces with crumpled wax paper.

Sister Susan remembers, "Rosettes and meringue cookies were stored in enamel pots (the kind used for canning and roasting), covered but not airtight. Sugar cookies and spritz were in Tupperware, as were Russian teacakes."

Russian teacakes, not my favorite and therefore a last resort when it came to sneaky snacking, were tucked into the large white rectangular bin. They shared space with the sugar cookies that Mom let us decorate. The sugar cookies were a hot item, and my greedy little hands knew how to maneuver the teacakes to take up more space in order to cover up the holes that tattled on the missing.

Spritz were also my favorite. Mom said they were putzy to make, but her efforts paid off. She used green dough to make perfect little pine trees and wreaths, decorated with red or green sugar. Yellow dough became stars, white dough camels, and pink dough poinsettias.

The pale green Tupperware contained the peanut butter cookies with the chocolate kisses pushed into the center — a double treat. A cookie AND a piece of candy? The person who invented that cookie was nothing short of brilliant.

More rosettes could be found in the large white-bottom Tupperware with a gold top that doubled in the off-season as a popcorn bowl. Another of my favorites, but because they were so large and covered in powdered sugar it was nearly impossible to sneak one without Mom noticing both the hole in the container and the powdered sugar dusting my face and shirt.

# Anise Cookies

Dalquist Family, Twin Cities, Minnesota

Mabel Dalquist, mother-in-law to Dorothy of Nordic Ware (see page 28), noted, "Tastes excellent, but clumsy looking cookies."

I adore this cookie and am excited to share the recipe. The anise flavor of this cloverleaf-shaped cookie is especially intense if you take a few minutes to heat the anise before adding it to the dough. To dispel Mabel's belief that Anise Cookies are clumsy looking, chill the formed dough for 30 minutes before popping it in the oven. This prevents spreading and keeps the cloverleaf design plump and intact.

1 ½ cups (3 sticks) butter, softened

1 cup sugar

2 egg yolks

1 teaspoon vanilla extract

3 cups flour

1 teaspoon baking powder

2 teaspoons anise seed, roasted in pan over medium-high heat until fragrant (about 2 minutes), then ground fine

½ teaspoon salt

In a large bowl, beat together butter and sugar until light and fluffy; stir in yolks and vanilla. Whisk together flour, baking powder, anise, and salt. Add flour mixture to butter mixture and stir until well combined. Form dough into small, teaspoon-size balls and place three balls together on a parchment-lined baking sheet, leaving about 2 inches between each cookie. Chill each sheet of cookies at least 30 minutes or up to an hour.

Preheat oven to 350 degrees. Bake cookies for 8 to 10 minutes or until edges turn brown. Inner cookies should remain relatively pale. Cookies are very delicate when warm. Let cool on baking sheet about 2 minutes before removing to a flat surface to cool.

**MAKES 40 COOKIES**

# Swedish **Butter Cookies**

Recipe by Inga Rude Olson, contributed by Kathy Weck, Farmington, Minnesota

I am a fan of any recipe that makes use of leftovers and what I've already got stashed in my pantry. Swedish Butter Cookies will use up any extra yolks from a recent egg boil (try them at Easter!). They are rich but not overly sweet and have a wonderful texture.

4 hard-boiled eggs, cooled

1 cup (2 sticks) butter, softened

½ cup sugar

¾ teaspoon almond extract

pinch salt

2 cups flour

colored sugar (optional)

Preheat oven to 400 degrees and line baking sheets with parchment paper. Peel eggs; separate yolks from whites; reserve whites for another use. Finely grate yolks or press through a sieve. Beat the butter and sugar until smooth. Beat in the egg yolks and the extract. Add salt, and slowly mix in the flour just until incorporated. Use a spritz-style cookie maker to press dough onto prepared baking sheets, or shape into balls using 2 tablespoons of dough and press slightly to flatten. Decorate with colored sugar if desired. Bake about 8 to 10 minutes.

**MAKES 36–42 COOKIES**

# Christmas Cookies

Adapted from a recipe provided by Dean E. Abrahamson, Minneapolis, Minnesota

With their cakey texture, these cookies remind me of dipping my hands
into the cookie jar as a kid and pulling out a perfect snack.

½ cup (1 stick) butter, softened

1 ½ cups packed brown sugar

2 tablespoons buttermilk

2 eggs, well beaten

3 cups flour

1 teaspoon baking soda

½ teaspoon ground nutmeg

½ teaspoon cinnamon

½ cup chopped nuts

1 cup raisins

1 cup currants

1 teaspoon orange zest

Preheat oven to 350 degrees and line baking sheets with parchment paper. Beat butter and brown sugar until light and fluffy. Add buttermilk and eggs; beat well. Add remaining ingredients and mix thoroughly. Shape into balls using 2 tablespoons of dough and place 2 inches apart on prepared baking sheets. Flatten slightly. Bake for 12 minutes or until golden brown and crisp. Remove from baking sheet and cool.

**MAKES 48 COOKIES**

# *Kokosnöt Drömmar* (Coconut Dreams)

Baker's ammonia, also known as ammonium bicarbonate and ammonium carbonate, is a leavening agent that predates baking soda and baking powder (which arrived on the baking scene in the nineteenth century). Baker's ammonia can be purchased from specialty baking and spice stores and online. Known for its powerful aroma (used as smelling salts for Victorian-era fainting ladies, presumably because a delicate female would rather revive than sniff that toxic odor), baker's ammonia is best used in low-moisture baked recipes, as the crisping process dries out the goodie and dissipates the baker's ammonia scent. Cookies and crackers that call for baker's ammonia are lighter than those that use baking powder or soda and do not hold the same soapy taste. However, you can substitute the more common leavener if desired.

Bitter almond extract is available in Sweden. If you or a friend is planning a trip to Scandinavia, be sure to request a bottle or two of this intense extract. Substitute it for almond extract, but use half the amount.

¾ cup sugar

½ cup (1 stick) butter, softened

1 cup flour

¼ teaspoon salt

½ teaspoon baking powder (or ammonium carbonate, preferred: see head note)

½ teaspoon almond extract (or ¼ teaspoon bitter almond extract, preferred: see head note)

¾ cup sweetened coconut flakes

Beat together sugar and butter until light; add remaining ingredients and mix until a smooth dough forms. Chill 1 hour. Preheat oven to 300 degrees. Roll dough into small, 1-inch balls and place on greased baking sheets. Bake for 18 to 20 minutes. Remove from pan while still hot; cool on a rack. Cookies will be quite delicate before cooling.

**MAKES 24 COOKIES**

To create this recipe for the greatest event on earth (THE MINNESOTA STATE FAIR!), I drew from several of my favorite resources, including a beloved Swedish Tabernacle Church cookbook, *Lussebullar*, our chubby ginger-colored cat Orson (aka Pinchy), and my daughter Stephanie's fanatical love of ginger.

One of my most cherished possessions is my great-aunt Hazel's copy of *Friendship League's Book of Tested Recipes: Collected Among Friends of the Swedish Tabernacle Church* from Minneapolis, Minnesota. This was the same cookbook Cindy Ostberg lent me after I interviewed her about Swedish food traditions (see page 22). At the time, I asked my great-aunt Hazel if she'd heard of the book. "No, no, I've never heard of such a thing!" Aunt Hazel told me.

Years later when she passed away, I found the forgotten cookbook in the bottom of a drawer in Aunt Hazel's kitchen, buried under dozens of cookbooks and recipe clippings from our local newspapers.

Now I keep the cookbook on a shelf and take it down often to thumb through the gray and yellow pages. The recipes are in that old style: ingredients listed and followed by brief (sometimes completely omitted) instructions for preparation. "Pin Wheel Cookies," credited to Mrs. Albin Johnson and Mrs. C. Arthur Rydell, is one of the few slightly complicated recipes that provides detail about assembling the cookies. I adjusted the chocolate and vanilla pinwheel recipe to suit Stephanie's ginger obsession by turning the chocolate layer into intense ginger and the vanilla layer into citrus. (I also added a pinch of cayenne pepper because there are two ingredients that Stephanie never leaves home without: ginger and Sriracha hot sauce.)

I didn't want to just roll the cookie and cut into circles. Circles didn't feel special enough. I looked to our cat Orson, nicknamed Pinchy because he has a sweet little pinched face, for inspiration. Orson was just coming off an amazing weight loss. When we adopted him, his weight was out of control and yo-yoing between twenty and twenty-five pounds. After a successful diet and exercise program, he eventually plateaued at seventeen pounds. His once obese frame was almost sleek, and when he curled into a ball he looked like a *lussebulle*, the S-shaped saffron buns Swedes serve at Lucia Day celebrations (see page 30). An S-shaped ginger cookie was born! 🦴

# Ginger Pinchies

2015 Minnesota State Fair Gold Medal Flour Cookie Contest Blue Ribbon winner

½ cup (1 stick) butter, softened

½ cup sugar

1 egg yolk, beaten

3 tablespoons milk

1 ½ cups plus 1 tablespoon Gold Medal all-purpose or unbleached flour

½ teaspoon baking powder

½ teaspoon salt

1 teaspoon vanilla extract

zest of 1 orange (about ½ teaspoon)

zest of 1 lemon (about ½ teaspoon)

2 tablespoons molasses

2–3 tablespoons grated fresh ginger (or 1 teaspoon ground)

¾ teaspoon cinnamon

½ teaspoon ground cloves

¼ teaspoon allspice

pinch nutmeg

pinch cayenne

Use a stand mixer with paddle or a hand mixer to beat butter on low speed for about 30 seconds. Gradually add sugar and beat on medium speed until fluffy, about 3 to 4 minutes. Turn mixer to low and add yolk; add milk and mix well. In small mixing bowl, whisk together 1 ½ cups flour, baking powder, and salt. Gradually add flour mixture and continue beating until dough forms.

Divide dough in half (there will be just over 2 cups total). Add half of the dough back to mixing bowl along with vanilla, orange zest, and lemon zest. Mix until incorporated. Form dough into ball and wrap in plastic; set aside. Place remaining dough in mixing bowl along with remaining 1 tablespoon flour, molasses, ginger, cinnamon, cloves, allspice, nutmeg, and cayenne. Mix until incorporated; dough will be very soft. Form dough into ball and wrap in plastic. Chill both dough balls at least 30 minutes.

Place parchment paper over work surface and roll each dough ball into a ¼-inch-thick, 8x5–inch rectangle. Place one dough rectangle over the other, aligning the dough as perfectly as possible. Starting at one of the narrow ends of the dough, use the parchment to gently roll the dough into a spiral, stopping a little more than halfway up the rectangle. Flip dough upside down and roll the other end into a spiral so that dough resembles an S-shaped log. Wrap in clean plastic and chill at least an hour.

Preheat oven to 350 degrees and line baking sheets with parchment paper. Slice chilled dough into ¼-inch-thick slices for about 16 S-shaped cookies. Place on prepared baking sheets about 1 to 2 inches apart. Bake for 8 to 10 minutes or until evenly browned on bottom. Cool on rack.

**MAKES ABOUT 16 COOKIES**

Ribbon cookies are similar to jam-filled thumbprint cookies, except that ribbons are baked in long strips, then filled with jam and cut into smaller bites. As I interviewed bakers about their Swedish cookie traditions, I collected three ribbon cookie recipes. They are similar and all delicious, but not identical.

## Grandma's **Raspberry Ribbons**

Carole Jean Anderson, Minneapolis, Minnesota

1 egg

¼ cup plus 1 tablespoon sugar

¾ cup (1 ½ sticks) butter, softened

1 teaspoon almond extract

2 ½ cups flour

1 teaspoon baking powder

¼ teaspoon salt

¾ cup seedless raspberry jam, stirred to loosen

1 cup confectioner's sugar

1 teaspoon vanilla extract (or use almond extract)

2 tablespoons buttermilk

Preheat oven to 375 degrees and line baking sheets with parchment paper. In large mixing bowl, beat together egg, sugar, and butter. Stir in 1 teaspoon almond extract. In separate bowl, whisk together flour, baking powder, and salt. Add flour mixture to batter and mix well.

Divide dough into 4 parts. Shape each section into long strips, about 16 inches long and 2 ½ inches wide. Transfer strips to prepared baking sheets, one strip per sheet. Use finger to make dent along center of each strip. Use small spoon or pastry bag to fill each indentation with raspberry jam.

Bake sheets one at a time for 8 to 10 minutes. Cookies will remain quite pale but become firm when baked. While cookies are still hot, use sharp knife to cut each strip diagonally into 1-inch diamond-shaped cookies. Cool.

Whisk together confectioner's sugar, 1 teaspoon vanilla or almond extract, and buttermilk. Drizzle cooled cookies with glaze.

**MAKES 60 COOKIES**

# Lena's **Christmas Cookies**

Lynn Moore, Bemidji, Minnesota

During a visit to Sweden in the 1980s, Florence Moore collected this recipe from Lena, who wrote the instructions in Swedish to share with Minnesota. Lynn Moore recalls:

"My mother in-law [Florence Moore] traveled to Sweden more than once. She loved these cookies, and Lena, a second cousin, wrote out the recipe complete with drawings depicting the rope [log] and a small dip in each piece to fill with jam. We added Lena's recipe to our holiday cookies. I had the original recipe minus the English translations but lost it one year. An exchange college student from Norway translated the recipe.

"I believe this recipe is similar to Jam-Filled Brussels Cookies, but we always call them Lena's Christmas Cookies. I entered the recipe in the annual cookie contest in Fort Myers, Florida. My recipe received the second most points, so it was part of the Bake Off. Now, it didn't win, but a photo of the cookie was featured on the front page of the paper, above the fold. I fill the dip with my homemade pin cherry jelly, and it remains brilliant red after baking, like a ruby."

14 tablespoons (1 ¾ sticks) butter, softened

½ cup sugar

1 teaspoon vanilla extract

2 cups flour

1 teaspoon baking powder

¼ teaspoon salt

¼ cup raspberry jam, stirred to loosen

Preheat oven to 350 degrees and line baking sheets with parchment paper. In large mixing bowl, beat together butter, sugar, and vanilla until well combined and fluffy. In small mixing bowl, whisk together flour, baking powder, and salt. Add flour mixture to batter and mix until well combined. Divide batter into 3 or 4 sections.

On clean work surface, roll each section into a rope about 16 inches long and 2 ½ inches wide. Use a clean, sharp knife to cut each rope into 1 ½–inch pieces. Transfer cookies to prepared baking sheet, about 1 to 2 inches apart. Use your finger to make a little dent in the center of each cookie, and fill each indentation with about ½ teaspoon of jam. Bake 10 minutes. Cookies will remain quite pale but begin to take on a bit of color when they are baked through.

**MAKES 20–25 COOKIES**

# Lingonberry Jam Cuts (*Syltkakor*)

Faye Olson, Brooklyn Park, Minnesota

**"We used to make them to sell at ASI [the American Swedish Institute]."**

1 cup (2 sticks) butter, softened

½ cup granulated sugar

1 teaspoon vanilla or almond extract

2 ¼ cups flour

1 ⅓ cups lingonberry or other seedless jam

1 cup confectioner's sugar

Preheat oven to 350 degrees and line baking sheets with parchment paper. In bowl of stand mixer, beat together butter and granulated sugar; stir in flavoring and flour. If mixer does not incorporate flour, use hands to knead it in on lightly floured board. Divide into 4 portions and roll each into a log about 16 inches long. Place each log on a prepared baking sheet and use a dowel or the handle of a wooden spoon to create an indent running the length of the log. Bake for 12 to 15 minutes.

Meanwhile, process jam until smooth. Set aside. Whisk together confectioner's sugar and a few drops water, vanilla, or almond extract until glaze forms. Glaze should be firm yet produce a thin drizzle.

Carefully remove logs from baking sheets and place on cutting board. While logs are still warm, run a thin stream of jam down the center indentations and drizzle with glaze (see tip). Cut into 1-inch pieces before cooling, wiping knife clean occasionally.

**MAKES 48 COOKIES**

 **TIP:** A plastic sandwich bag with corner cut off is a good instrument for applying jam and glaze.

# Amelia's *Fattigman* (*Klenäter*)

Adapted from Amelia Erickson Westman recipe provided by
Dean E. Abrahamson, Minneapolis, Minnesota

My Swedish aunties set out trays and trays of beautiful cookies at Christmas. When it was time for dessert I reached for every treat I could balance on my plate until a stern look from my parents stopped me. *Fattigman* (poor man's cookies) were strange and wonderful, shaped like terrifying sea monsters I imagined whenever I listened to my Disney album *20,000 Leagues Under the Sea*.

While *fattigman* is the common Norwegian term for these fried cookies, in Sweden they are also known as *klenät* (cruller), *klena* (thin, weak), and *kleyna* (slender, possibly frail).

6 egg yolks

1 egg white

¼ cup plus 2 tablespoons granulated sugar

¼ cup plus 2 tablespoons heavy cream

2 tablespoons brandy

3 cups flour

½ teaspoon baking soda

½ teaspoon salt

lard for frying

confectioner's sugar

Beat egg yolks and white well. Mix in sugar, cream, and brandy. In a separate bowl, whisk together flour, baking soda, and salt. Beat flour mixture into batter to make a stiff but very sticky dough. Wrap in plastic wrap and refrigerate 4 hours or overnight.

Work in small batches to roll dough on lightly floured surface into squares ⅛ inch thick. Use special cruller cutter or scissors to cut into long diamond-shaped strips, about 1 by 3 inches. Cut slit in center and fold ends through hole (see below).

Heat lard to 350 degrees; deep-fry cookies about 1 minute each side. Remove cookies from hot lard when they are golden brown. Place on cooling racks over brown paper. Sprinkle with confectioner's sugar when cool.

**MAKES 34 COOKIES**

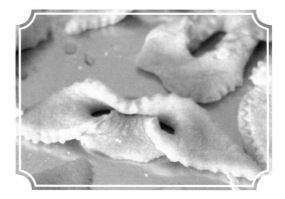

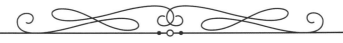

My mother's Christmas meringue cookies (colored red or green and dotted with chocolate chips or nuts) were one of the first cookies I reached for on the Christmas cookie tray.

I loved their delicate airiness and crunch. That's probably why I am endlessly intrigued with meringue cookies and cakes of all varieties. Swedes also refer to meringue cookies as *marängviss*, and the Danes have their own version, called kisses (*kys*).

*Hovdessert* is a Swedish meringue cookie that I first read about in my ancient copy of Time-Life's *Cooking of Scandinavia*. In Swedish, *hov* means royal and hoof. This cookie is supposedly named for the court, yet the first few times I made it, it looked very hoof-like. The *Cooking of Scandinavia* recipe includes a simple chocolate sauce, but when a student in one of my cooking classes mentioned her grandmother's hard sauce, I was inspired to create a balsamic version.

# *Hovdessert* (Swedish Royal Meringues with Chocolate Balsamic Sauce)

Winner of Minneapolis *Star Tribune* 2012 Holiday Cookie Contest

**For the cookies**

4 egg whites, at room temperature

⅛ teaspoon cream of tartar

pinch salt

1 cup superfine sugar

2 tablespoons unsweetened cocoa powder, sifted or whisked to remove lumps

Preheat oven to 250 degrees and line baking sheets with parchment paper.

In a bowl of a stand mixer with whisk attachment, beat egg whites, cream of tartar, and salt on medium-high speed until mixture is foamy. Gradually add sugar and continue beating until egg whites are very stiff and form solid peaks when the whisk is lifted out of the bowl, at least 5 minutes. Using a rubber spatula, carefully fold in cocoa powder.

Fill a pastry bag fitted with a star tip (or a plastic bag with a corner cut out) with batter and pipe basket-shaped circular cookies, 1½ inches wide and 1½ inches tall, with a small indented opening in the center (or make a tiny depression in tops of cookies with wet finger or back of wet spoon). Or use a small scoop to drop mounds of batter onto prepared baking sheets and make the indentations on top.

Bake until cookies are dry and crisp on the outside but tender on the inside, 50 to 60 minutes. If cookies start to take on any color, reduce heat to 200 degrees. Remove from oven and cool 5 minutes before transferring cookies to a wire rack to cool completely.

**For the sauce**

3 ounces dark chocolate

⅓ cup heavy cream

¼ cup packed brown sugar

1 tablespoon balsamic vinegar

2 tablespoons cold butter

1 teaspoon vanilla extract

In small saucepan over low heat, combine chocolate, cream, and brown sugar, stirring occasionally until chocolate has melted. Stir in vinegar. Remove from heat; stir in butter until melted. Stir in vanilla extract and cool slightly. Spoon sauce into center of cooled cookies.

**Other sauce combinations:** chocolate peppermint (swap out the vinegar for 1 teaspoon peppermint extract and decorate with crushed peppermint candies); mocha (swap out the vinegar for 2 teaspoons instant coffee crystals); almond (swap out the vinegar for 1 teaspoon almond extract). Add a teaspoon or two of cream if the sauce is too thick.

**MAKES ABOUT 24 COOKIES**

# Hazelnut Kisses

4 egg whites, at room temperature

⅛ teaspoon cream of tartar

pinch salt

1 cup superfine sugar

4 ounces whole hazelnuts, skins removed (see tip), plus more for serving

1 cup white chocolate chips

3 tablespoons heavy cream

2 teaspoons coarse or flaked salt (optional)

Preheat oven to 250 degrees and line baking sheets with parchment paper. Prepare meringue as with *Hovdessert* (page 53), omitting cocoa powder. Use a small ice cream scoop or tablespoon to place small round cookies on prepared baking sheets. Push 1 whole hazelnut into the center of each cookie. Bake for 40 to 50 minutes. Cool cookies completely. Roughly chop remaining hazelnuts and set aside.

In small saucepan over very low heat, melt chips and cream together. When mixture is just melted but not hot, pour into pastry bag with uncut tip. Cut tiny hole in tip and decorate tops of cookies with lines of chocolate. Sprinkle with additional chopped nuts and salt if desired.

**MAKES ABOUT 40 COOKIES**

  **TIP:** To remove skins from hazelnuts, bring 3 cups of water and 3 tablespoons baking soda to boil in a small saucepan. Add hazelnuts and boil 3 minutes. Drain, then use clean kitchen towel to wipe skins from nuts.

# Lemon Meringue Kisses

4 egg whites, at room temperature

⅛ teaspoon cream of tartar

pinch salt

1 cup superfine sugar

¾ cup prepared lemon curd

lemon zest (optional)

Preheat oven to 250 degrees and line baking sheets with parchment paper. Prepare meringue as with *Hovdessert* (page 53), omitting cocoa powder, piping onto prepared baking sheets, and baking as directed. When cookies are cool, fill each indentation with a teaspoon or two of the curd. Garnish with lemon zest if desired.

**MAKES ABOUT 24 COOKIES, DEPENDING ON SIZE**

# Peppermint Kisses

4 egg whites, at room temperature

⅛ teaspoon cream of tartar

pinch salt

1 cup superfine sugar

5 tablespoons crushed hard peppermint candy, divided

2 tablespoons coarsely chopped white chocolate chips

Preheat oven to 250 degrees and line baking sheets with parchment paper. Prepare meringue as with *Hovdessert* (page 53), omitting cocoa powder. Gently fold in 3 tablespoons of peppermint candy and the chips. Use a small ice cream scoop or tablespoon to place small round cookies on prepared baking sheets. Sprinkle tops with remaining candy. Bake for 40 to 50 minutes. Cool cookies completely.

**MAKES ABOUT 40 COOKIES**

 **NOTE:** Start small with the amount of dough used for each cookie, as they expand in the oven. These cookies store well in the freezer, and their flavor and texture are even better the second day.

# Grandma's **Kringlers** (Cookies)

Recipe by Ellida Viktoria Erickson Johnson, contributed
by her granddaughter Joann Lowrie, Becker, Minnesota

"Grandma's best cookie recipe, the one we all adored
and still make today EVERY CHRISTMAS."

5 cups flour

1 cup sugar, plus more for sprinkling

5 teaspoons single-acting baking powder

1 teaspoon baking soda

1 cup (2 sticks) butter, softened

4 ounces (½ cup) lard

5 egg yolks

1 ½ cups sour cream

1 teaspoon vanilla extract

1 ½ teaspoons almond extract

Preheat oven to 350 degrees. Mix flour, 1 cup
sugar, baking powder, and baking soda in a
large bowl. Add butter and lard and blend
with a pastry blender or two forks until the
size of small peas. Add yolks, sour cream, and
flavorings; use hands to mix thoroughly, then
chill. Make walnut-sized balls and roll them on
a floured board to make ropes about ¼ inch
thick and 6 inches long; form the ropes like a
pretzel. Dip tops in sugar and bake until golden
brown, about 12 minutes.

**MAKES 96–120 COOKIES**

The Norwegians claim so many Christmas cookies that it is almost impossible to bake a cookie with pure Swedish American roots, from *sandbakkel* to *fattigman*. *Krumkake* is another. They are so delicious that they appear in many Christmas cookie presentations, regardless of country of origin.

They are easy to make, but you will need a special *krumkake* griddle. The griddles—electric or for stovetop—are indented with round decorated forms that shape the cookies from both sides as they cook, like a waffle iron. Once cooked and still hot, the *krumkake* are shaped into tubes.

There are two types of *krumkake* batter. One is loose, like a thick pancake batter. The other is thick, like a waffle batter. The loose batter forms an airy, crisp cookie, while the thicker batter forms a denser cookie.

Cooled *krumkake* can be eaten as is, sprinkled with powdered sugar, used as ice cream cones, or filled with sweet cream and berries (as the Danes serve them).

The first few times I attempted *krumkake*, I invited my friend Kathryn to help. She was raised with Norwegian baking traditions, so I didn't feel too guilty when, as it was time to take the hot cookies off the griddle to form into cones, I claimed helplessness and giggled nervously as she burned her fingers while rolling each cookie. Years later I learned from the Nordic Ware crew to remove the cookies from the griddle with a kitchen knife, then roll the cookie around a wooden dowel, pressing firmly against a flat surface. The technique has saved my fingers.

# Krumkake

Barbara Scottston, formerly of Anoka, Minnesota

"The product is more like batter than dough. A later update increased the cinnamon and suggested 1 ½ teaspoons ground cardamom for the seeds. Usually two or three *krumkake* irons were in use concurrently. Cone shapes were not used to form the tube-shaped cookies; a wooden stick or fat knitting needle formed them."

I demonstrated this recipe for customers at the Nordic Ware store in St. Louis Park, Minnesota. The consensus was that these cookies reminded many of us of a famous cinnamon toast–flavored cereal. They are light and crisp, and your kitchen will smell like cinnamon for days after making them.

4 eggs

1 cup sugar

1 cup (2 sticks) butter, melted

1 cup heavy cream

1 tablespoon cinnamon

about 20 cardamom seeds, ground with mortar and pestle

2 cups flour

Beat eggs until very light and add sugar, melted butter, cream, flavoring, and flour.

Preheat the *krumkake* iron until a drop of water sizzles when dropped onto the top. Open the iron; coat lightly with nonstick spray. Spoon 1 teaspoon of batter onto center of the hot iron. Close iron. Bake about 1 minute on each side until the cookie is lightly browned. Insert the tip of a knife under the cookie to remove from the iron; roll the hot cookie into a cigar or cone shape (see page 57). Cool on a rack. Cookies become crisp as they cool. Repeat with remaining batter. Batter will thicken as you use it; add water a tablespoon at a time as necessary to thin it to the consistency of thick cream. Store the baked cookies in an airtight container.

**MAKES ABOUT 60 COOKIES**

# Coconut Cardamom *Krumkake*

One holiday season I forgot to buy cream for my *krumkake*. I found a can of coconut milk in the pantry and created these cookies. They remind me of lotus flower blossom cookies that can be found at our local Hmong restaurants.

1 cup sugar

½ cup (1 stick) butter, melted

2 eggs

1 cup full-fat canned coconut milk

½ teaspoon vanilla extract

1 teaspoon freshly ground cardamom

1 ½ cups flour

In a medium bowl, beat together the sugar with the butter, then whisk in eggs until the mixture is light and lemon colored. Whisk in milk, vanilla, cardamom, and flour until smooth. Let stand 30 minutes.

Preheat the *krumkake* iron until a drop of water sizzles when dropped onto the top. Open the iron; coat lightly with nonstick spray. Spoon 1 tablespoon batter onto center of the hot iron. Close iron. Bake about 1 minute on each side until the cookie is lightly browned. Insert the tip of a knife under the cookie to remove from the iron; roll the hot cookie into a cigar or cone shape. Cool on a rack. Cookies become crisp as they cool. Repeat with remaining batter. Batter will thicken as you use it; add water a tablespoon at a time as necessary to thin it to the consistency of thick cream. Store the baked cookies in an airtight container. They can be kept frozen for several weeks.

**Optional flavors** to replace or add to cardamom: ¼ teaspoon almond extract; zest from lemon, lime, or orange.

**MAKES ABOUT 24 COOKIES**

# *Mandel Kranze* (Almond Wreath Cookies)

From Ellen Arvidson as provided by Carole Jean Anderson, Minneapolis, Minnesota

1 cup plus 2 tablespoons sugar

1 ⅓ cups chopped blanched almonds, divided

1 teaspoon cinnamon

1 cup (2 sticks) butter, softened

2 eggs

zest of 1 lemon

2 cups flour

1 egg white, whisked but not beaten

Preheat oven to 400 degrees and line baking sheets with parchment paper. In small mixing bowl, combine 2 tablespoons sugar, ⅓ cup chopped almonds, and cinnamon. Set aside.

Beat butter and gradually beat in remaining 1 cup sugar. Add whole eggs, one at a time, beating well after each addition. Add zest, flour, and remaining 1 cup almonds. (If dough is too soft too handle, refrigerate for 20 minutes.) For each cookie, form a ball with 1 to 1 ½ inches (about 2 teaspoons) of dough. On a lightly floured board, roll out each ball into a 3-inch rope and form into wreath shapes, gently pressing ends together.

Arrange wreaths 1 inch apart on prepared baking sheets. Brush with egg white and sprinkle with sugar, almond, and cinnamon mixture. Bake about 8 minutes or until lightly browned and crisp.

**MAKES 56 COOKIES**

# Orange Almond **Melting Moments**

Finalist in Minneapolis *Star Tribune* 2013 Holiday Cookie Contest

The first time I came across a melting moment cookie recipe was when I was speaking with a woman named Daisy who kept insisting I take a copy of her handwritten recipe card: "You must try the melting moments." Daisy, a proud Swedish American living in Minneapolis, insisted the cookies were Swedish. I've never found evidence to their Scandinavian heritage, but I haven't found any evidence against their possible roots, either.

After my visit with Daisy I started seeing recipes for melting moments everywhere, often with different names: Italian Butter Cookies, Swedish Cornstarch Cookies, Melt Aways, and Melt-In-Your-Mouths.

This recipe revives the traditional melting moments with modern flavors. I added almond and orange to mimic the flavors of the Danish pastry my mom makes every Christmas morning, while the heat from the chipotle pepper felt like a natural way to soften the sweetness.

≻⪍ ⪎⪌

1 cup flour

⅔ cup cornstarch

¼ teaspoon ground chipotle chile

¼ teaspoon salt

1 cup (2 sticks) butter, cut into tablespoons, softened

⅓ cup confectioner's sugar

freshly grated zest of 1 orange

½ teaspoon almond extract

In a large bowl, whisk together flour, cornstarch, ground chipotle chile, and salt. Set aside.

In bowl of a stand mixer, beat butter on medium-high speed until creamy, about 1 minute. Add confectioner's sugar, orange zest, and almond extract, and beat until light and fluffy, about 2 minutes. Reduce speed to low, add flour mixture, and mix until a grainy dough forms. Use hands to shape dough into a ball. Wrap dough in plastic wrap and refrigerate for 30 to 60 minutes.

Preheat oven to 325 degrees and line baking sheets with parchment paper. Roll dough into tablespoon-sized balls and place 2 inches apart on prepared baking sheets. Bake 12 to 14 minutes: cookies will be very light colored; do not overbake. Remove from oven and cool 5 minutes before transferring cookies to a wire rack to cool completely.

### For the icing

3 tablespoons freshly squeezed orange juice

1 tablespoon butter, softened

1 teaspoon almond extract

1 teaspoon vanilla extract

¼ teaspoon salt

2 ¾ cups confectioner's sugar

½ cup raw sliced almonds for serving

freshly grated orange zest for serving (optional)

In bowl of a stand mixer, beat orange juice, butter, almond extract, vanilla extract, and salt on medium speed until creamy. Reduce speed to low, add confectioner's sugar, and mix until smooth. Using a small spatula or knife (or a pastry bag), glaze cookies. For a less sweet cookie, use only 1 teaspoon icing; for a sweeter cookie, glaze liberally. Garnish with almonds and orange zest, if desired.

**MAKES 24 COOKIES**

# Swedish Hugs

Carol Sime, St. Paul, Minnesota

"This traditional Christmas cookie has become a family favorite of mine. It came from my childhood neighbor and appeared in a Lutheran church cookbook with the usual cryptic directions. I have not found either the name or the exact recipe online; the recipe is one that has been handed down in a Swedish American family for generations.

"My former neighbor LaVonne Peterson Behr now lives in Arizona. I thought this cookie was worthy of sharing for two reasons: It has the lovely aroma and taste of the Swedish favorite spice, cardamom. Vikings first encountered the spice in what is now Turkey when Constantinople was the bridge between Asia and Europe. [And] my source for the recipe, the Peterson family, was instrumental in the moving of Gustavus Adolphus College from East Union, near Red Wing, Minnesota, to St. Peter, Minnesota, in 1876. LaVonne's great-grandfather used his influence and money to relocate the college. All of LaVonne's aunts and uncles attended Gustavus, and [her great-grandfather] Andrew's picture hung in Old Main."

These are pretty cookies, filled with flavor and crunch. Swedish Hugs complete me (and my Christmas cookie tray).

2 cups (4 sticks) butter, softened

2 cups packed brown sugar, plus more for rolling

1–2 eggs

1 teaspoon vanilla extract

1 cup almonds, chopped

2 teaspoons cinnamon

2 teaspoons ground cardamom

1 teaspoon baking powder

3 ½ cups flour

1 cup whole blanched almonds

Preheat oven to 375 degrees and line baking sheets with parchment paper. In large mixing bowl, beat together butter and sugar until light and fluffy. Add 1 egg and vanilla and beat until well combined. In separate bowl, whisk together chopped almonds, spices, baking powder, and flour. Add flour mixture to batter and mix well. Roll into balls the size of a walnut. If desired, beat remaining egg; dip cookies in egg and then in sugar. Place on prepared baking sheets about 1 inch apart. Place a blanched almond on top of each cookie round. Bake for 8 to 10 minutes, until golden brown and crisp outside.

**MAKES 60 COOKIES**

# Pepparkakor
Carole Jean Anderson, Minneapolis, Minnesota

1 cup (2 sticks) butter, softened

1 ½ cups sugar

1 egg

1 teaspoon light corn syrup

3 cups sifted flour

2 teaspoons baking soda

2 teaspoons cinnamon

2 teaspoons ground ginger

½ teaspoon ground cloves

1 tablespoon orange zest

Beat together butter and sugar; add egg and corn syrup and beat well. Sift dry ingredients and mix into batter. Add zest and mix well. Divide dough into 2 balls and wrap in plastic wrap. Chill 4 hours or overnight.

Preheat oven to 400 degrees and line baking sheets with parchment paper. On lightly floured surface, roll dough ⅛ inch thick. Cut into desired shapes. Place on prepared baking sheets and bake 5 to 6 minutes or until just beginning to crisp. Cookies will continue to crisp as they cool.

**MAKES SEVERAL DOZEN COOKIES, DEPENDING ON SIZE**

# Pepparkakor
Faye Olson, Brooklyn Park, Minnesota

"My grandmother's. I sometimes just make small balls and flatten with a glass. These keep well in a covered tin."

1 ½ cups (3 sticks) butter, softened

2 cups sugar

1 cup molasses

1 ½ tablespoons ground ginger

1 ½ tablespoons cinnamon

1 tablespoon ground cloves

1 ½ cups whipping cream, whipped

1 tablespoon baking soda dissolved in 1 tablespoon water

9 cups flour

In a very large mixing bowl, beat together butter and sugar. Add molasses and spices, blending gradually. Add whipped cream and baking soda dissolved in water; mix in flour until well blended. Cover and let stand overnight.

Preheat oven to 375 degrees and line baking sheets with parchment paper. Knead dough and divide into manageable pieces. On a lightly floured board, roll each piece very thin. Cut dough into desired shapes and place ¾ inch apart on prepared baking sheets. Bake for 7 to 9 minutes. Cool on rack.

**MAKES ABOUT 300 SMALL COOKIES**

# Spicy *Pepparkakor* (thin and crisp gingersnaps)

Adapted from recipe published in *Saveur* (2009), from Vete-Katten bakery in Stockholm

3 ¾ cups flour

3 teaspoons ground cloves

3 ½ teaspoons ground cinnamon

½ teaspoon ground nutmeg

½–1 teaspoon cayenne

1 ¼ teaspoons baking soda

11 tablespoons butter, softened

1 cup packed dark brown sugar

¼ cup molasses

¼ cup dark corn syrup

2 tablespoons freshly grated orange zest

½ cup heavy cream

Sift together flour, cloves, cinnamon, nutmeg, cayenne, and baking soda; set aside. In a large bowl, beat together the butter, brown sugar, molasses, corn syrup, and orange zest until mixture is pale and fluffy, 1 to 2 minutes. Add reserved flour mixture and heavy cream in 3 alternating batches, beginning and ending with flour mix, mixing until the dough just combines. Divide dough in half and shape each half into flat disk. Wrap disks in plastic wrap; refrigerate at least 1 hour.

Preheat oven to 350 degrees and line baking sheets with parchment paper. Unwrap 1 disk and place on floured work surface. Roll dough to ⅛-inch thickness. Cut out cookies using cutters of choice and place 2 inches apart on prepared baking sheets. Repeat with remaining dough, re-rolling scraps (see tip).

Bake cookies, 1 sheet at a time, until browned and set, about 12 minutes. Transfer to rack and cool completely before decorating.

Frost with your favorite icing, if desired. **To make a simple glaze,** combine confectioner's sugar with a bit of almond extract and juice from an orange or lemon or freshly grated ginger.

QUANTITIES VARY ACCORDING
TO SIZE OF COOKIE CUTTER

 **TIP:** Keep scraps in a separate mixing bowl and refrigerate at least 20 minutes before reshaping and rolling. Work slowly and in batches to get the best results.

# Rosettes

Susan Johnson Schmitt, Gaylord, Minnesota

"I've always drained the cookies on newspaper, probably because that's how it's always been done. Besides, it's cheap and doesn't leave [paper towel] fuzz on the cookies."

Regarding the use of lard versus oil,

"Again, that's how it's always been done. I usually do half Crisco and half lard. Cookies have a better taste if oil isn't used. Remind folks to reheat the iron after every three or four cookies."

Susan is my sister, and the family's rosette master. I always heed her advice when it is time to take out the iron and heat the lard.

2 eggs, beaten

1 tablespoon sugar

⅛ teaspoon salt

1 cup flour, sifted before measuring

1 cup milk or half-and-half

2 tablespoons butter, melted

lard and vegetable shortening for frying

confectioner's sugar

In large mixing bowl, whisk together eggs, sugar, and salt. Whisk in flour, alternating with milk and butter, until smooth batter forms. Cover and refrigerate for 2 hours.

To a large Dutch oven or deep fat fryer, add equal parts lard and vegetable shortening to a depth of 1 to 1 ½ inches; warm to 350 degrees. Heat rosette iron in oil. Tap off excess grease from iron and dip iron into batter; do not allow batter to rise above top of iron. Dip battered iron into hot grease. If rosette does not release from iron, use a knife to remove cookie and drop it into fat (see tip). Flip rosette to cook both sides, about 30 to 60 seconds each side. When rosette is golden brown, use a spider or slotted spoon to remove rosette from fat and drain on paper (newspapers or paper bags). Dust cooled rosettes with confectioner's sugar.

**MAKES 48 COOKIES**

 **TIP:** If iron is too cool, the batter will slip off into the fat. If iron is too hot, the batter will stick. Heat iron again, and repeat process, remembering to stir batter each time.

# Sandbakleser

Adapted from Mrs. C. Arthur Rydell's recipe in *Friendship League's Book of Tested Recipes*

*Sandbakleser* (known as *sandbakkel*s in Norwegian, translated as sand tarts) are a delicate cookie, made by shaping dough into the bottoms of small tin shells that resemble tiny tart pans. The cookies are eaten plain, sprinkled with sugar (and occasionally cinnamon sugar), or as a fancy dessert filled with whipped cream and fruit preserves.

1 cup (2 sticks) butter, softened

1 cup sugar

1 egg

2 cups flour

½ teaspoon almond extract

Preheat oven to 375 degrees. Beat together butter and sugar. Add egg, flour, and extract and mix until well combined. Place cookie tins on baking sheet and lightly spray each tin with nonstick cooking spray. Form a tablespoon of dough into a ball and form on the outside of crinkle tins (or press into the center of tin). Press thinly and evenly onto sides and bottom. Chill 15 minutes. Bake for 10 minutes or until tarts are golden brown. Cool, then tap gently on tins to remove cookies. The cookies are very delicate and break easily.

**MAKES 42 COOKIES USING 1 ½–INCH TINS**

# Kristine Mortensen

## MY CHRISTMAS COOKIE STORY

I was inspired to bake by my mother, who was a terrific baker, cook, and hostess. I was also inspired by my aunt Martha, another woman who excelled at the domestic arts and also had a career—a rare combination when I was growing up in the 1950s and early '60s. My mother worked in the trust department of a bank. Aunt Martha was a home economist with the Wisconsin Electric Power Company in Milwaukee, and for many years was involved in the production of its annual "cookie book" and popular holiday cookie show. I still have several editions of the book, first published in 1928.

My mother's Christmas cookie repertoire included spritz, rosettes, pecan tarts, *sandbakkel*se, and, of course, cutout sugar cookies that my sister and I had the honor of frosting. She also made lefse, cardamom bread, and cloverleaf dinner rolls for the holidays, along with apple, pumpkin, and pecan pie!

I didn't begin developing my own Christmas baking repertoire until I lived in Sweden in the 1970s and '80s and discovered the Scandinavian connection to many of the holiday baked goods I had enjoyed since childhood in Wisconsin.

The cookies I bake today for my family are primarily from recipes I acquired in Sweden, and when I asked my now adult children, who were born in Sweden, to tell me which are their favorites, they both named the same two: *havreformar* and *skurna knäckkakor*.

*Havreformar* are a rustic version of almond tarts made with oatmeal in addition to almonds. I use the smaller forms, about 2 inches in diameter at the top, which yield a perfect, two-bite cookie. *Skurna knäckkakor* are toffee shortbread slices, excellent for dunking in coffee.

Like my mother and other serious holiday bakers, I bake in marathon sessions, usually over one or two evenings. I added *skurna knäckkakor* to my repertoire several years ago because it's an easy cookie to make, in contrast to the fussy but showy *havreformar*. Both are attractive additions to any cookie plate.

# *Havreformar* (Oatmeal Almond Tarts)

The following recipes adapted from two pamphlets of cookie recipes Kristine collected while in Sweden, "Små Kakor" and "100 Kakor" (see page 68)

1 ¼ cups regular oatmeal

¼ cup raw, unpeeled almonds

⅔ cup butter, softened

¼ cup plus 2 tablespoons sugar

1 ½ cups pastry flour

⅜ teaspoon salt

Preheat oven to 365 degrees. Lightly coat inside of 30 *sandbakkelse* (small fluted tart) forms with nonstick cooking spray (see tip). Crumble the oatmeal slightly in your hands. Process nuts in food processor or use nut grater to create a medium- to fine-textured meal. Blend all ingredients together first using electric mixer at low speed for 1 minute and then finishing by hand to form a dough. Push a walnut-size clump of dough into each form, work dough up the sides, and trim excess off the top of the form with fingers. Bake on large baking sheet 10 to 12 minutes. Allow cookies to cool before carefully removing them from the forms (see tip).

**MAKES 30 COOKIES**

 **TIP:** To avoid making a mess, place the forms on a large baking sheet or jellyroll pan lined with paper towels before spraying. Remove paper towels before baking! If necessary, gently pinch the form and/or use the point of a small, sharp knife to release the baked cookie.

# *Skurna Knäckkakor*
## (Swedish Toffee Shortbread Slices)

When I tested this recipe, I ate half of the batch before it was completely cooled. It was important to rid the house of the remaining cookies immediately so that I didn't finish them all. These are the best cookies I've ever tasted. They have a dense texture with a hint of toffee. You have been warned.

¼ cup raw, unpeeled almonds

½ cup (1 stick) butter, softened

½ cup sugar

1 tablespoon light or dark corn syrup

1 ½ teaspoons vanilla extract

1 teaspoon baking powder

1 ½ cups pastry flour

¼ teaspoon salt

Preheat oven to 350 degrees and line baking sheets with parchment paper. Process nuts in food processor or use nut grater to create a medium- to fine-textured meal. Blend all ingredients together, first using electric mixer at low speed for 1 to 2 minutes and then finishing by hand to form a dough. Divide into 2 to 3 equal parts. Using hands, roll each into a log 10 to 12 inches long, place on prepared baking sheets, and flatten into a rectangle. Bake for 12 minutes. While still warm, use a dough scraper to cut each rectangle diagonally into thin slices.

**MAKES 50 COOKIES**

# Spritz

Dean E. Abrahamson, Minneapolis, Minnesota

*"Spritzkakor—the Swedish verb for pressing through a pastry bag or cookie press is att spritsa. Spritz were a Christmas favorite for mother—and for her family."*

If desired, add green, red, or yellow food coloring while mixing the dough. Spritz cookies do best when pressed directly onto a clean, unlined, ungreased baking sheet. Take your time: one batch, one sheet at a time. This is not a cookie to make if you are in a hurry. Always use a clean baking sheet. Chill dough before pressing onto the baking sheet, but if dough refuses to press out neatly, allow dough to set at room temperature for five minutes or until it is cool enough not to spread while baking but warm enough to be pliable and release easily from the press. Experiment with flavors you like: replace almond extract with orange or lemon. Decorate with colored sugar, diced candied fruit, citrus zest, or almonds.

1 cup (2 sticks) butter, softened

½ cup sifted confectioner's sugar

1 egg yolk

1 teaspoon almond extract

2 tablespoons ground blanched almonds

2 cups sifted flour

Preheat oven to 375 degrees. Beat together butter and sugar; beat in egg yolk and almond extract. Stir in ground almonds and flour a little at a time until dough is smooth and not too firm. Shape with cookie press onto clean baking sheet (see head note). Bake for 8 to 10 minutes or until golden yellow. Let cookies cool on cookie sheet.

**MAKES 45 COOKIES**

# Gerda's **Swedish Cookies** (Spritz)

Jackie Johnson, Woodbury, Minnesota

"This spritz recipe has been in my family forever! I remember both my grandmother and mother making them. When Mom gave me the recipe after I married, I found out it was from Aunt Gerda. I remember walking to her apartment when I was really little, and I also remember she always had cookies to share. My mom said that Aunt Gerda was the best baker in the family, high praise from a great baker!

"I belonged to several Swedish groups, and we made this recipe to sell at *Svenskarnas Dag*. And we only had to make it one time because it makes enough to feed a large party!"

3 cups sugar

2 cups (4 sticks) butter, softened

1 cup lard

2 eggs plus 1 egg yolk

2 teaspoons almond extract

6 cups flour

Preheat oven to 375 degrees. Beat together all ingredients until well blended. Shape with cookie press on clean baking sheets (see head note page 72). Bake for 6 to 8 minutes.

**MAKES 96–108 COOKIES**

# Almond Bread (*Mandelbröd*)

Carole Jean Anderson, Minneapolis, Minnesota

When I saw this recipe, I was intrigued. The dough is more like a cookie than a bread, and I wanted to include a quick bread among all of the yeast and ginger loaves. Carole Jean's Almond Bread is light and crisp, and a nice addition to a breakfast or dessert tray.

1 whole egg plus 1 egg yolk

⅔ cup sugar

½ cup (1 stick) butter, softened

1 ¾ cups flour

1 teaspoon baking powder

1 teaspoon almond extract

Preheat oven to 375 degrees and line a baking sheet with parchment paper. Beat together whole egg, yolk, and sugar. Mix in remaining ingredients. Shape into 2 logs, about 2 ½ inches in diameter. Place 2 inches apart on prepared baking sheet, and bake about 25 minutes or until centers are set. Breads will spread slightly. Cool for 15 minutes, and use serrated knife to cut into ½-inch slices.

**MAKES 24 SLICES**

# Swedish **Flatbread**

Gustavus Adolphus College, St. Peter, Minnesota

"This recipe is served as a signature bread offering at Gustavus. Sometimes herbs are added to make a more savory flatbread. Some patrons use butter—some do not. Courtesy Chef Paul (Jake) Jacobson and his Swedish heritage (Grandma's recipe book!)."

This bread is crisp and light, with a sweetness that pairs well with butter, cheeses, and fruit.

¼ cup (½ stick) butter

¼ cup sugar

8 ½ ounces flour (a little more than 1 cup)

¼ teaspoon salt

¼ teaspoon baking soda

¼ cup buttermilk

¼ cup heavy cream

Preheat oven to 350 degrees and line baking sheets with parchment paper. In small saucepan melt butter over low heat and add sugar. Stir until sugar is dissolved, then remove from heat. In a large mixing bowl mix together flour, salt, baking soda, buttermilk, and cream. Stir in butter and sugar mixture. Use stand mixer with dough hook (or hand knead) until well incorporated.

Divide dough in half and roll each portion out on floured surface into ¹⁄₁₆-inch (or thinner) sheets (see tip). Place on prepared baking sheets and bake for 8 to 10 minutes or until lightly brown. Let cool, then break into pieces. Store in airtight container and use in a day or two—or freeze for up to 3 months.

**SERVES 12**

  **TIP:** The common lefse rolling pin, with its ridges or crisscross pattern, works best with most flatbread recipes. If you are unsure about investing in a new rolling pin, try a batch or two with a regular pin. The bread may not roll as thin, but you will still have fine flatbreads and crackers.

# Kaarin's Grand Champion **Hard Tach**

Nancy Anderson and Kaarin Anderson Mantz, Cambridge, Minnesota

Nancy's family has been making this hard tach (crisp bread) for years. The family has carefully guarded the recipe, but Nancy was kind enough to share it for this project. It was one of the first recipes Nancy taught her daughter Kaarin to make, and Kaarin eventually won a 4-H grand championship at the Isanti County Fair and a blue ribbon at the Minnesota State Fair.

Kaarin, 2004 queen of Svenskarnas Dag, the annual Swedish Celebration Day that takes place a week after Midsummer at Minnehaha Falls in Minneapolis, is now teaching her own daughter the secrets to the family's cherished recipe.

"Making Hard Tach always signified the holiday season for me, and I loved giving it to family and friends as gifts. It is still one of my favorite holiday traditions that I am now passing down to my young daughter. She even has her own mini version of a hard tach rolling pin.

"When it came to 4-H, I knew it wasn't something that most people have made or know about, so it was an easy decision to submit that as one of my entries that year. I was so excited seeing that I won grand champion at our county fair and that I got to go on to the state fair. The judges at the state fair were impressed with the slightly sweet taste and thin and crispy consistency."

3 cups all-purpose flour

1 cup whole wheat flour

¼ cup wheat germ

1 cup lightly packed brown sugar

½ teaspoon salt

½ cup rolled oats

1 cup (2 sticks) cold butter

1 teaspoon baking soda

1 ½ cups buttermilk

Preheat oven to 350 degrees. Mix the flours, wheat germ, brown sugar, salt, and oats well and then cut in the butter using a pastry blender (or pulse in food processor) until the mixture resembles small crumbs. Dissolve the baking soda in the buttermilk and add to dry ingredients. Stir with wooden spoon and then mix with hands.

Divide dough into 8 portions. Knead each portion on a floured board and use a hard tach (or regular; see tip page 75) rolling pin to roll out to 11- to 12-inch rounds, about 1/16 inch thick. Transfer to a baking sheet and bake for 15 to 20 minutes or until light brown. Cool on wire rack. Break into serving pieces. Store in a loosely covered box or a covered cake pan.

**MAKES 8 ROUNDS**

# Good Old-Fashioned **Gingerbread**

Dalquist Family, Twin Cities, Minnesota

Since my introduction to this Dalquist family favorite, I've made this loaf many times. It uses a few common pantry ingredients and bakes into a soft, flavorful bread. Serve warm with butter, or top with lemon curd and whipped cream.

1 cup flour

¼ teaspoon salt

¼ teaspoon baking soda

¼ teaspoon cinnamon

¼ teaspoon ground ginger

¼ cup vegetable oil

¾ cup sugar

1 egg

¼ cup dark molasses

½ cup buttermilk

Preheat oven to 350 degrees and grease an 8x4-inch loaf pan (see note). Sift together flour, salt, baking soda, cinnamon, and ginger. In large mixing bowl stir together all ingredients and pour into prepared loaf pan. Bake for 25 minutes, or until inserted toothpick comes out clean.

**MAKES 1 SMALL LOAF, 6 SERVINGS**

  **NOTE:** If you select a smaller pan, you will have a higher loaf, and you will want to keep an eye on the loaf as baking time may vary. Test for doneness as instructed.

# Swedish **Holiday Bread**

Dean E. Abrahamson, Minneapolis, Minnesota

1 packet (2 ¼ teaspoons) active dry yeast

¼ cup warm water

1 cup milk, scalded (see tip page 12)

½ cup sugar

2 teaspoons salt

½ cup (1 stick) butter, softened

5 ½–6 cups sifted flour

2 eggs, beaten

1 ½ teaspoons ground cardamom

¼ teaspoon mace

1 cup raisins

**Glaze**

1 cup plus 2 tablespoons sifted confectioner's sugar

2 tablespoons hot water

1 teaspoon butter

Soften yeast in ¼ cup warm water. In a mixing bowl, stir together scalded milk with sugar, salt, and ½ cup butter; cool to lukewarm. Stir in about 2 cups of the flour, add eggs, and beat well. Stir in softened yeast. Stir in cardamom, mace, raisins, and remaining flour to make a soft dough. Turn out on a lightly floured surface and knead until smooth and elastic, about 8 to 10 minutes. Place in lightly greased bowl, turning once to grease surface. Cover and let rise in warm place until doubled in size, about 1 ½ hours. Punch down. Divide and round the dough into 2 balls, one for each braid. Cover and let rest for 10 minutes.

For each braid, divide 1 of the balls into thirds. Shape into strands 15 inches long, tapering the ends. Line up the strands 1 inch apart on a lightly greased baking sheet. Braid loosely without stretching the dough, beginning in the middle and working toward each end. Seal ends well. Cover and let rise in warm place until doubled, about 45 minutes. Bake at 350 degrees for 25 to 30 minutes.

Mix confectioner's sugar, 2 tablespoons hot water, and 1 teaspoon butter until well blended; drizzle over warm braids.

**MAKES 2 BRAIDS**

# Limpa

My limpa recipe combines every flavor I seek in this sweet rye bread with the addition of orange, the citrus that screams *jul*.

¼ cup very loosely packed brown sugar

2 tablespoons dark molasses

¾ cup warm water

1 packet (2 ¼ teaspoons) active dry yeast

1 teaspoon salt

1 ¼ cups medium (not coarse) rye flour

2–3 cups all-purpose flour

2 tablespoons butter, softened

zest of 1 orange

1 teaspoon ground anise

1 teaspoon ground fennel

1 teaspoon ground caraway

**Egg wash**

1 egg yolk

1–2 tablespoons freshly squeezed orange juice

1 teaspoon fennel seeds

1 teaspoon caraway seeds

In large mixing bowl, combine brown sugar, molasses, warm water, and yeast and allow yeast to rise until foamy, about 5 minutes. Stir in salt, rye flour, and enough of the all-purpose flour to make a dense but pliable dough. Knead in butter, zest, and ground spices. Add a bit of oil to a clean bowl and roll ball of dough in oil. Cover and let rise to double in size (this may take as long as 6 hours).

Gently shape dough into oblong loaf. Place on buttered baking sheet or in buttered 8x4–inch loaf pan; cover and let rise to double, about 2 hours.

Preheat oven to 375 degrees. Use sharp knife to slash a few parallel cuts across top of loaf. Whisk together egg yolk and orange juice; brush over top of loaf and sprinkle with seeds. Bake until bread is a deep golden brown and sounds hollow when tapped, about 30 to 40 minutes. Remove from oven and cool on rack at least 30 minutes.

**MAKES 1 LOAF**

# **Limpa** (Rye Bread)

From Albertha Sundstrom (Kansas), mother of Patty Karstadt and maternal grandmother of Bruce Karstadt, Minneapolis, Minnesota

This recipe results in a tender, delicate crumb with a subtle sweet flavor. Shape the loaves free form or use regular bread loaf pans.

2 cups warm water

4 cups all-purpose flour, divided

1 packet (2 ¼ teaspoons) active dry yeast

½ cup dark molasses

¼ cup sugar

1 ½ cups medium (not coarse) rye flour

½ teaspoon salt

¼ cup shortening

1 teaspoon ground anise

oil or butter for brushing

In large bowl beat together water, 2 cups all-purpose flour, and yeast. Mix in remaining 2 cups all-purpose flour and molasses, sugar, rye flour, salt, shortening, and anise and knead until soft, pliable dough forms. Place in large, well-greased bowl and cover with plastic wrap or clean kitchen towel. Let rise until doubled in size, up to 6 hours.

Shape dough into 2 loaves and place in well-greased 8x4-inch loaf pans. Cover with plastic wrap or kitchen towel. Let rise until doubled.

Preheat oven to 350 degrees. Bake loaves for 1 hour, covering with foil for final 10 minutes. While bread is still hot, brush tops with oil or melted butter.

**MAKES 2 LOAVES**

# Almond Rusks (*Mandelskorpar*)

Faye Olson, Brooklyn Park, Minnesota

---

**"From my dear friend Doris, who has passed away."**

Faye's recipe for rusk is easy to bake, beautiful to present, and delicious to eat. The combination of almond extract and toasted ground almonds packs a wallop of almond flavor and texture. Leave at least three inches between loaves during the first bake, as the bread spreads quite a bit.

1 cup sugar

1 cup (2 sticks) butter, softened

2 eggs

1 teaspoon almond extract

¼ cup sour cream

1 teaspoon baking powder

½ teaspoon baking soda

¼ teaspoon salt

3 ½ cups flour

½ cup ground almonds, toasted

Preheat oven to 350 degrees and line baking sheets with parchment paper. Beat together sugar and butter; beat in eggs and almond extract. Stir in remaining ingredients, reserving about ½ cup flour. Mix thoroughly, adding additional ½ cup flour if dough is too wet to shape. Divide dough into 2 pieces; form each piece into a log 12 inches long, 2 inches wide, and 3 inches tall. Transfer logs to prepared baking sheets (see tip) and bake for 20 minutes. Cool at least 30 minutes or until cool to the touch.

Reduce oven temperature to 200 degrees. Cut logs into ½-inch-thick slices and lay flat on parchment-lined baking sheets, about half an inch apart. Bake in batches about 25 minutes. Carefully flip each piece and continue baking for an additional 25 minutes. Slices will appear dry and golden.

**MAKES ABOUT 40 (3-INCH) COOKIES**

---

 **TIP:** Brush an egg wash on logs and sprinkle with raw or sanding sugar before baking.

# Rusk (Swedish Toast)

Carla Grant Adams, Golden Valley, Minnesota

> "Swedish Toast is a double baked cookie with cardamom and almonds.
> It is delicious and a good coffee-dunker."

These rusk are reminiscent of zwieback. They are a very dense toast with beautiful dark caramel color. Use them in Swedish Meatballs (page 124) and Apple *Kaka* (page 169).

1 cup (2 sticks) butter, softened

2 cups sugar

2 eggs, beaten

3 ½ cups flour

½ teaspoon salt

2 teaspoons baking powder

1 cup Greek-style yogurt

2 teaspoons crushed cardamom seeds

1 cup coarsely ground almonds

Preheat oven to 350 degrees. Mix all ingredients together in large bowl. Batter will be thick. Line a 9x13–inch cake pan with parchment paper; grease paper and dust with flour. Spread the batter evenly on the bottom of the pan. Bake for 40 to 50 minutes, or until golden brown and inserted toothpick comes out clean. Cool overnight (this is essential).

Preheat oven to 275 degrees. Remove cake from pan. Remove parchment paper and slice cake lengthwise into three equal loaves. Cut each loaf into ½-inch slices. Place slices, cut side down, on parchment-lined baking sheets. Bake until lightly browned and crisp, about 45 minutes.

**MAKES 48–60 COOKIES**

# Swedish **Rye Bread**

Faye Olson, Brooklyn Park, Minnesota

2 cups water

¼ cup plus 2 tablespoons packed brown sugar

1 tablespoon salt

1 packet (2 ¼ teaspoons) rapid-rise yeast

2 tablespoons shortening

¼ cup molasses

2 cups medium (not coarse) rye flour

4 cups all-purpose flour

In large mixing bowl, beat together all ingredients except 3 cups of the all-purpose flour. Move dough to lightly floured board and gradually knead in remaining flour until pliable, silky dough forms. Form a ball and place in large, well-oiled mixing bowl. Cover bowl with plastic wrap or clean kitchen towel and let rise until doubled in size, about 1 ½ to 2 hours.

Gently shape into 2 loaves; place in greased 8x4–inch loaf pans, cover with plastic wrap or towel, and let rise until doubled in size, about 1 hour.

Preheat oven to 375 degrees and bake for 30 to 45 minutes or until loaf sounds hollow when tapped. Cool and remove from loaf pans.

**MAKES 2 LOAVES**

# Swedish **Rye Bread**

Susan Swanson, Mahtowa, Minnesota

Susan reports that the original recipe came from Mrs. Lambert (Edna) Dahlsten,

> "my parents' dearest friend: she had a *jul* open house for some professors and families, and this was a favorite of mine. She was a voice professor, and her husband an organ professor.

> "This is a must for my daughter and grandkids. They love it toasted with cream cheese. It makes great sandwiches with meatballs or ham. I've made this since I was first married (forty-six years ago), as I liked it better than my grandmother's recipe, which is like this but with no caraway or orange."

This recipe makes a sturdy, slightly sweet loaf, perfect for toasting. Try it topped with herring salad, gravlax, or avocado.

1 cup medium (not coarse) rye flour

2 ¾–3 ¼ cups all-purpose flour, divided

1 cup buttermilk

½ cup mashed potato plus ½ cup water that potato boiled in, at room temperature

1 packet (2 ¼ teaspoons) active dry yeast

¼ cup packed brown sugar

¼ cup molasses

2 tablespoons butter

¼ teaspoon crushed caraway seeds, plus more for topping

zest of 2 oranges

1 teaspoon salt

1 egg yolk (optional)

1 tablespoon orange juice (optional)

Combine rye flour, ¼ cup all-purpose flour, buttermilk, potato and water, and yeast thoroughly in large mixing bowl. Cover with plastic wrap and let rise until doubled in size, about 2 hours.

In saucepan, stir together brown sugar, molasses, butter, caraway seeds, zest, and salt. Bring to boiling and then cool. Add mixture to dough, and knead in 2 ½ to 3 cups all-purpose flour, adding only as much flour as needed to make a silky, somewhat wet dough. Form into loaf and set into a very well-buttered 8x4–inch loaf pan (or free form the dough and place on well-buttered or parchment-lined baking sheet). Cover with plastic wrap and let rise until doubled in size.

Preheat oven to 375 degrees. If desired, use a sharp knife or razor blade to make parallel slices on top of bread and brush with egg yolk mixed with orange juice. Decorate with a few teaspoons of caraway seeds. Bake for 40 minutes or until bread sounds hollow when tapped and is a rich golden brown.

**MAKES 1 LOAF**

# Doug's Swedish **Rye Bread**

Dalquist Family, Twin Cities, Minnesota

---

2 tablespoons salt

⅓ cup shortening

1 cup packed brown sugar

½ cup molasses

2 packets (4 ½ teaspoons) active dry yeast

1 teaspoon granulated sugar

4 cups medium (not coarse) rye flour

8–9 cups all-purpose flour

Add 4 cups water, salt, shortening, brown sugar, and molasses to large stockpot and bring to boil. Cool to 110 degrees.

In small bowl, proof yeast by stirring together ½ cup warm water, yeast, and granulated sugar. Set aside for about 5 minutes or until foam develops.

In very large mixing bowl, stir together cooled brown sugar–molasses mixture with proofed yeast mixture. Stir in rye flour and 7 cups all-purpose flour so that a sticky dough forms. Knead in up to 2 additional cups all-purpose flour so that dough is easy to handle. Knead until a smooth dough develops, about 10 minutes. Place dough in clean, very large mixing bowl coated lightly with vegetable oil. Roll dough in oil so that all sides are coated. Cover bowl with plastic wrap and set in warm, draft-free area until doubled, 2 to 3 hours.

Gently fold dough over itself and reform ball. Place back into oiled bowl and cover with plastic wrap for second rise until doubled, about 2 hours.

Gently divide dough into 4 equal pieces. Shape into loaves and place in greased 8x4–inch loaf pans. Cover with plastic wrap and let rise until doubled in size, about 2 hours.

Preheat oven to 375 degrees. Slash tops of loaves with razor blade or sharp knife. Bake until loaves sound hollow when tapped, about 35 minutes.

**MAKES 4 LOAVES**

# Gustie envy in a rye loaf

I've always had a mean case of Gustie envy. Maybe it's the success so many Gustavus Adolphus graduates find, maybe it's the post-graduate allure of small college versus big state university life, or maybe, just maybe, it's the food.

Gustavus Adolphus College, a small liberal arts college rooted in Swedish and Lutheran heritage, was founded in 1862 by Swedish Americans in Red Wing, Minnesota. The college later moved to St. Peter, where it continues to lure students from across the globe.

I'd heard plenty about Evelyn Sponberg Young, mostly humorous tales about Ma (as she was affectionately called by the Gusties lucky enough to know her) and her driving (she was a notorious speeder who allegedly collected numerous tickets while driving from her home in a Minneapolis suburb to the St. Peter campus) and her enthusiastic support of the Gustavus basketball team that her husband coached (was she really booted from games because of the insults she hurled at refs?). Young, a Gustavus alumna, earned her legendary status while running the Gustavus dining hall, where she reigned for thirty years as the manager of food service.

Young regulated the meals as well as where they were eaten. Playwright and storyteller—and former Gustie—Kevin Kling recalls run-ins with Young, especially a time when he attempted to smuggle food out of the cafeteria for a student meeting:

I was so busted. She was not happy. I was way more afraid of her than anyone in administration; her driving habits alone were legendary. I explained the situation and she looked at what I had taken and said, "Well, that won't be near enough." Then she proceeded to load me up with food for the meeting and to feed my roommate and me for the rest of the week. Bread, a head of lettuce, a huge chunk of bologna that I don't think would fit in carry-on luggage at the airport.

She always smiled at me after that like we had pulled off a caper together. And I guess we had.

Legends never die, and Young's memory lives on not just in the stories told about her but in her recipes, many of which appear in her cookbook, *All This . . . and Rye Bread, Too*. It wouldn't be a stretch to admit that the lure of writing a book about Swedish *jul* included an opportunity to gush about the recipe for Evelyn "Ma" Young's rye bread. I buy a few loaves every year from the Gusties who sell it at the American Swedish Institute's Midsommar celebration in Minneapolis, but a stash of Young's rye in my freezer doesn't always cut it when cravings hit.

Gustavus Adolphus generously contributed many of their recipes to this project, including Ma's rye bread, page 88.

# Swedish **Rye Bread**

Gustavus Adolphus College, St. Peter, Minnesota

"This recipe is served as a signature bread offering at Gustavus. Recipe courtesy
Ms. Evelyn Young, longtime Gustavus dining service director and quite an amazing
personality. Evelyn was known regionally and nationally for her hospitality, energy,
and generous spirit, and the college (and the world today) is a better place for her
gift of love . . . 'and rye bread too'!"

1 cup milk

1 cup water

2 ½ tablespoons vegetable shortening

½ cup molasses

¼ cup plus 1 tablespoon granulated sugar

¼ cup packed brown sugar

1 teaspoon salt

1 teaspoon anise oil or ground anise

2 packets (4 ½ teaspoons) active dry yeast

¼ cup warm water

2 cups medium (not coarse) rye flour

4–5 cups all-purpose flour

melted butter for brushing

Scald milk (see tip page 12); transfer to large mixing bowl and stir in water, shortening, molasses, ¼ cup granulated sugar, brown sugar, salt, and anise. Dissolve yeast in warm water with remaining 1 tablespoon sugar. When milk mixture has cooled but is still warm to touch, stir in yeast, then rye flour, and mix until smooth using a stand mixer with dough hook or a strong arm and a wooden spoon. Add white flour bit by bit until dough is easy to handle but still a bit sticky. Turn dough out onto floured board and knead until smooth, about 10 minutes. Place in a greased bowl and let rise in a warm place until doubled in size, about 1 hour.

Divide dough into 3 portions and shape into balls. Cover and let rest 15 minutes. Flatten, roll, and tuck ends to form loaves and place in well-greased (8 ½ by 4 ½–inch) loaf pans. Let rise in a warm place until doubled, about 30 minutes. Preheat oven to 375 degrees and bake for 30 to 35 minutes. After removing from oven, brush generously with melted butter and turn out of pans onto cooling rack.

**MAKES 3 LOAVES**

# Rye Puffs

These puffs make great appetizers for any holiday party. I pair them with ice-cold locally produced aquavit. Serve with lingonberries or sour cream and inexpensive roe; garnish with chives and dill.

1 cup water

½ cup (1 stick) butter

1 cup medium (not coarse) rye flour

1 teaspoon ground caraway

zest of 1 orange

pinch salt

4 eggs

24 (quarter-inch) cubes Västerbotten or similar cheese (or use your favorite aged cheese with nutty flavor, preferably with grainy crystals)

In saucepan over medium-high heat, bring water and butter to boil; simmer until butter melts. All at once add rye flour, caraway, orange zest, and salt and continue heating, stirring with wooden spoon until mixture forms a ball. Remove from heat and let cool about 3 to 5 minutes. Use a wooden spoon to beat in eggs one at a time; beat until dough is smooth.

Preheat oven to 400 degrees. On ungreased baking sheet lined with parchment paper, use a small ice cream scoop or pastry bag to shape dough into puffs about 3 to 4 tablespoons in size, set 3 inches apart. Push a cube of cheese into each puff and gently reshape puff around cheese. Bake 35 to 40 minutes or until puffed and golden.

**MAKES 24 SMALL PUFFS**

# Swedish **Tea Ring**

Nancy Anderson, Cambridge, Minnesota

This recipe originated with Nancy's grandmother and her sister Connie Lindberg.

> "Advice from Grandma Larson: She told me when she first taught me to bake a tea ring that when you bake any bread be sure that you treat the dough with love when kneading it and it will be perfect every time!"

This tea ring is a showstopper. The instructions for shaping the wreath may appear complicated, but once you understand how to make the cuts and twist each cut, the shaping is actually quite easy.

## For the dough
1 packet (2 ¼ teaspoons) active dry yeast

¼ cup warm water

1 cup milk

¼ cup granulated sugar

¼ cup shortening

1 egg, beaten

¾ teaspoon salt

3 ½ cups flour

## For the filling
3 tablespoons butter, softened

⅓ cup packed brown sugar

3 teaspoons cinnamon

## For the frosting
1 tablespoon warm milk

¾ cup sifted confectioner's sugar

1 teaspoon almond extract

In small bowl, dissolve yeast in water. In saucepan, heat 1 cup milk until not quite boiling. Remove from heat and cool to 110 degrees. In large mixing bowl, combine granulated sugar, shortening, egg, and salt. Stir in milk and yeast. Use a wooden spoon to stir in 1 ½ cups flour (or use stand mixer with dough hook). Let rest 5 minutes. Bubbles should appear on surface of dough.

Mix in remaining flour. If dough is too sticky, add up to ½ cup more flour while kneading. Dough should be easy to handle but not stiff. Form dough into ball and place in greased bowl. Cover with plastic or clean kitchen towel and let rise in warm place until dough is doubled in size, about 1 hour.

Lightly grease a baking sheet. On lightly floured surface, roll dough into a 10x20–inch rectangle. If dough does not maintain its shape, cover it with plastic or towel and let rest for 5 minutes or until it is pliable. Spread surface with butter, brown sugar, and cinnamon. Carefully roll the dough up lengthwise and transfer, seam side down, to prepared baking sheet. Form dough into a circle on the baking sheet, seam side down, by connecting the ends together.

Use a sharp knife or kitchen shears to cut dough at 1-inch intervals, about three-quarters deep. Fold each cut in alternating directions so that every other section is twisted in the opposite direction of the cut above and below it. Fan slices out from and into the center of the ring. Cover the roll with greased plastic wrap and let rise until doubled in size, approximately 45 minutes to 1 hour.

Preheat oven to 375 degrees. Bake for 30 minutes, until golden brown. Cool. Whisk together 1 tablespoon warm milk, confectioner's sugar, and almond extract and use to frost tea ring.

**MAKES 1 RING**

The way Carolyn Ruff describes her family legacy involves a little bit of luck, some romance, and plenty of hard work. As all good chocolate stories do.

Carolyn's namesake and grandmother Caroline Erickson came to America from Torsby Bada, Värmland, on a "terrible boat" when she was two years old. Caroline was nearly dropped overboard by an uncle, which, as Carolyn wrote in her young adult novel *Keystones of the Stone Arch Bridge*, "would've made for an abrupt ending to my family's story!"

The Ericksons arrived in Minnesota in the mid-1880s and settled along the river flats, an area on the west bank of the Mississippi River in Minneapolis. This haphazard, diversely populated neighborhood was named for whichever immigrant group happened to live there at any given time, thus Danish Flats, Cabbage Patch, or Bohemian Flats. Caroline's family eventually moved up and out of the flats to west of downtown Minneapolis. Their home was large enough for the family to take in boarders.

Carolyn's great-grandfather Per Edward "Ed" Pearson immigrated alone to America from Bergsattra, Värmland, in Sweden when he was twelve years old. He boarded with the Ericksons, and when he found a house in the same neighborhood, Ed sent for his family, including his four brothers.

Ed and Caroline eventually fell in love and married. They raised their family in Minneapolis, where Ed became such a successful candy salesman that he traded in his horse and buggy for the Model T Ford he drove across the region.

The Pearson family gathered on their front porch on hot summer afternoons, often taking turns stirring melted chocolate as it cooled into candy. The family's candy was so delicious that Ed realized he could make his own confections rather than distribute someone else's. The Pearson Candy Company was born on that front porch in 1909, and Pearson's brothers soon joined his efforts as the company grew into a regional empire.

Pearson's Candy Company introduced Nut Goodies in 1912. The chocolate-covered peanut and cream bars flavored with the distinctly northern ingredient of maple became an iconic regional treat. Salted Nut Rolls joined the lineup twenty-one years later, and today a variety of candies claim the Pearson's name. While the family hasn't owned the company since 1969, the Pearson's Candy Company continues to operate in the Twin Cities at the same St. Paul location where it's been since 1959.

Carolyn Ruff's grandmother Caroline wrote this description of Christmas in Sweden: "In Maria Finson's home, Christmas was a huge celebration, lasting from Christmas Eve until the twentieth of January. Maria said that during this time, 'nobody lifted a finger,' but the preparation for this period began months in advance. During this period, everyone walked to church each day for services and church was a Swedish mile from home. This may not seem too great a hike except that she said the Swedish mile was equivalent to seven American miles!"

The Pearson family continues to celebrate Christmas with the traditions passed down through the generations, from *Yulekage* (*Julkaka*) to berry pudding and cream. Of course, a Pearson family Christmas dessert isn't complete without a generous serving of candy. ✍

Pearson Family *Yulekage* (page 94)

# Pearson Family *Yulekage*

Caroline and Per Pearson's granddaughter, Carolyn Ruff

"Our family's traditions have evolved over time. Our *Yulekage* has become an ode to cardamom with the addition of caramel sauce and pecans (no citron) and always shaped into an open braided wreath."

If a pan of gooey caramel pecan rolls and cardamom bread had a baby, this would be the result: the best of both worlds in a festive wreath-shaped loaf.

1 yeast cake or 1 packet
(2 ¼ teaspoons) active dry yeast

¼ cup plus 1 teaspoon granulated sugar

½ cup warm water

1 cup milk, scaled and cooled to 110 degrees

½ cup (1 stick) butter, softened

¾ teaspoon salt

2 eggs

16 cardamom pods, shells removed and seeds crushed with an electric grinder or mortar and pestle

4 cups flour, sifted

**For the caramel sauce**

1 cup packed brown sugar

6 tablespoons (¾ stick) salted butter

½ cup heavy cream

1 teaspoon salt

**For the filling**

6 tablespoons (¾ stick) butter, softened

½ cup packed brown sugar

1 cup chopped pecans

**For topping**

pecan halves

colored sugars for sprinkling

In small mixing bowl, dissolve yeast and 1 teaspoon granulated sugar in warm water. In separate small mixing bowl, combine cooled milk, ½ cup butter, ¼ cup granulated sugar, and ¾ teaspoon salt. In a large mixing bowl, beat eggs. Add yeast mixture, milk mixture, cardamom, and 2 cups sifted flour, mixing thoroughly. Add remaining 2 cups sifted flour and mix thoroughly. Transfer dough to a floured surface and knead 6 to 8 minutes, until pliable and silky.

Place dough in large well-greased bowl and cover with wax paper and kitchen towel. Let rise until doubled in size, about 1 to 1 ½ hours, then gently reshape into new ball and return to bowl. Cover with wax paper and kitchen towel and let rise to double again, about 1 hour.

In a heavy saucepan, whisk together 1 cup brown sugar, 6 tablespoons salted butter, heavy cream, and 1 teaspoon salt. Bring to simmer without stirring. Cool. Divide among 4 pie tins.

Transfer dough to floured surface and divide into 4 pieces. Roll out each piece of dough to an 8x11–inch rectangle. Spread each portion evenly with softened butter, brown sugar, and chopped pecans. Roll lengthwise into a rope, twist to form a wreath, and place in prepared pie tin. Decorate top of wreath with pecan halves and sprinkle with red and green sugar. Set aside to rise for 1 hour.

Preheat oven to 350 degrees and bake for 30 minutes. Cool, then add a ribbon bow before serving

**MAKES 4 WREATHS**

# Nut Goodie Wannabes

If you can't find Pearson's Nut Goodies in your area, give my dad's recipe a try. This recipe and similar ones are all over the internet and in community cookbooks. They vary a bit, but all of them call for the combination of semisweet chocolate, butterscotch, and peanuts.

My dad was not exactly a master cook, but he did do a few things really well. Like frying frozen burritos in butter. Or frying Swedish meatballs in butter. Or frying lefse in butter. You get the idea. He wasn't much of a baker, so I was surprised when he started making homemade batches of Nut Goodie Wannabes. Similar to the Pearson patriarchs, my dad quickly mastered the art of chocolate-covered peanuts and maple cream. Nut Goodies were his favorite holiday snack—and his contribution to our Christmas cookie tray.

12 ounces semisweet chocolate chips

12 ounces butterscotch chips

2 cups peanut butter

1 ½ cups salted peanuts

1 cup (2 sticks) butter

1 (3-ounce) package vanilla pudding mix (not instant)

½ cup evaporated milk

1 teaspoon pure maple extract

2 pounds confectioner's sugar

In large saucepan, melt chocolate and butterscotch chips and peanut butter over medium-low heat, stirring constantly. Spread half in a 10x15–inch jelly roll pan and let set until firm. Stir the peanuts into the remaining portion of melted chips and set aside.

In clean saucepan, melt butter and stir in pudding mix and milk; bring to boil and simmer 1 minute. Add extract and beat in confectioner's sugar until smooth. Spread over set layer. Top with chocolate-peanut mixture. When firm, cut into bars.

**MAKES 60–72 BARS (UNLESS YOU SLICE THEM AS LARGE AS MY DAD USED TO)**

# Yulekaka

Faye Olson, Brooklyn Park, Minnesota

2 cups milk, warmed

½ cup (1 stick) butter, melted and cooled to under 110 degrees

½ cup sugar

1 teaspoon cinnamon

1 teaspoon freshly ground cardamom

½ teaspoon salt

1 egg

1 packet (2 ¼ teaspoons) rapid-rise yeast

6 cups flour

2 cups mixed dried fruit

½ cup raisins plumped in ⅓ cup rum or water (see tip)

In very large mixing bowl, combine milk, melted and cooled butter, sugar, spices, salt, egg, and yeast with 3 cups of flour. Beat well; add remaining flour, fruit, and raisins (drain and squeeze rum out of raisins and set rum aside: see tip); knead until pliable dough forms. Form into ball. Place dough ball in large greased mixing bowl. Cover with plastic wrap or clean kitchen towel and let rise until doubled in size, 1 to 2 hours.

Shape into 2 long, narrow loaves and place on parchment-lined baking sheets. Cover and let rise until doubled in size, about 1 hour.

Preheat oven to 350 degrees. Bake for 45 to 50 minutes. Cool completely. Sift tops with confectioner's sugar or glaze if desired (see tip).

**MAKES 2 LOAVES**

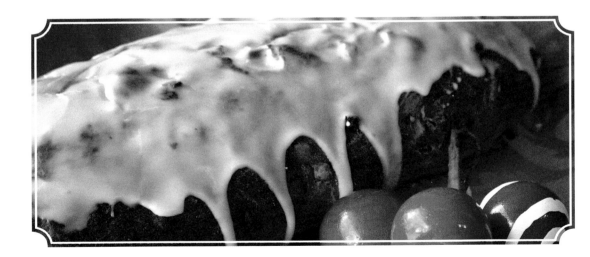

 **TIP:** Rum is my addition. Make a raisin-rum glaze by whisking 1 cup confectioner's sugar with 2 tablespoons raisin-soaking rum until well combined. Pour glaze over cooled loaves.

I met Dean Abrahamson when his grandson and I were students in a Swedish language class at the University of Minnesota. I was writing my master's thesis on Swedish immigration and food traditions, and Dean agreed to let me interview him in his home.

Years later, I still recall wearing my favorite white jeans, not knowing that Dean's friendly black cats Carl and Karin (named for the Larssons, the Victorian-era artists who depicted a comfortable, romantic lifestyle raising their many children in a quaint Swedish cottage) would show me the kind of affection my own cats reserve for the person who feeds them. I left Dean's house with a trove of recipes and black fur–coated white pants.

Dean generously shared his cookbook, *Mother's Recipes*, an epic volume that includes hundreds of recipes collected by his mother, Evelyn Anna Trogen Abrahamson, as well as contributions from Dean and other family and friends. *Mother's Recipes* is one of those rare labors of love that is a balance of nostalgia and expertise. Dean included many of the notes Evelyn penciled on to her collection of recipe cards, including modifications and tips.

Among the cookies, cakes, breads, hot dishes, and soups are several thin bread recipes that intrigued me. Evelyn's people were from Dalarna, where the preparation of *tunnbröd* is an art.

I come from a family that—while we may enjoy the floury flat potato breads of Scandinavia (most especially Norwegian lefse)—doesn't actually take the rolling pin to the dough. I am a self-taught lefse maker (and not a very able one). However, the promise of Swedish flatbread was too appealing to ignore, and soon I was kneading rye and barley flour with cooked potatoes and rolling the dough into cute little Texas and Florida shapes. While not the prettiest rounds ever made, they certainly were delicious.

I began sharing the Abrahamson flatbread recipes with students in my cooking classes, referring to them as Swedish lefse. So easy, even a Swede like me can make them; so delicious, even the Norwegians will partake!

I owe Dean much, as *Mother's Recipes* is a text I return to often. The recipes within it record one hundred years of Swedish Minnesota kitchen history.

# Soft Dalarna Thin Bread (*Tuttul*)

This bread, buttered while still hot and rolled around soft cheese, or sliced potatoes and *surströmming*, or fried herring, is a delicacy.

2 ½ pounds cooked potatoes (see tip), peeled and chilled

1 teaspoon salt

2 scant cups coarsely ground rye flour

Mash or rice potatoes. Knead together potatoes, salt, and flour to a stiff dough. Divide dough into 10 pieces and roll out paper thin. Cook on both sides in dry, medium-hot skillet or on a griddle.

**MAKES 10 PIECES**

# Thinbread (*Tunnbröd*)

1 ¼ pounds cooked potatoes (see tip), peeled and warm

1 cup barley meal

pinch salt

flour for rolling

Grate or rice the warm potatoes. Place in bowl of stand mixer with dough hook and mix in barley meal and salt (or mix by hand). Divide dough into 10 parts and, working on a floured surface with a floured rolling pin, roll each into a very thin circle. Prick dough on both sides and cook in a hot, dry skillet for about 2 minutes each side. Let bread cool on wire rack covered with a cloth. Freeze or store in plastic bags.

**MAKES 10 PIECES**

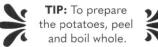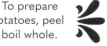
**TIP:** To prepare the potatoes, peel and boil whole.

# Swedish **Thin Bread**

Michelle Hals, North Branch, Minnesota

"I use about ⅔ cup of dough to yield those results."

2 cups milk

1 cup heavy cream

1 ¼ teaspoons baking powder

½ teaspoon salt

1 cup wheat germ

1 cup oatmeal

2 ½–3 ½ cups flour, plus more for rolling

Preheat oven to 425 degrees. Mix together all ingredients to form stiff dough. Divide into 8 portions. Using a corrugated rolling pin on a floured surface, roll out a portion of dough until thin, about 12 inches in diameter. Place on dry baking sheets and bake until golden brown, about 16 to 20 minutes.

**MAKES 8 FLATBREADS**

 **TIP:** Wrapping baked flatbreads in a flour sack or white dish towel helps to dry them out and make them crisp.

# three

## LUTFISK SUPPERS
## & CHURCH
## BASEMENT TALES

## ALL I really need to know about life, I learned from lutfisk.

**1. You are the smell, and happiness often follows discomfort.**

Finding Day Fish Company isn't difficult. However, identifying the tiny fishery is slightly complicated. Turn off the highway where a handful of farmhouses dot the two- or three-block stretch along a back road outside of Braham proper. Locate the debilitated gray former creamery on the corner (if it is still there), and next to it is a small brick one-story building with a faded "Day Fish" sign. You'll know you are in the right place during lutfisk season (October through February) and during store hours because a half dozen cars and SUVs will line the street and makeshift parking lot. Regulars (which describes most of the folks you'll meet) march up to the entrance (it's the door blinged out with tattered lye fish bumper stickers).

Walking into Day Fish is a ramble back in time, like going down into your grandparents' musty cement basement when you were a kid. It's dark, dank, and overwhelming with the fragrance of lye-soaked cod. Never smelled uncooked lutfisk? Imagine a heavy aroma: powdered perfume and chemical rot. Aquatic with a rich, choking presence. Lutfisk doesn't have a smell so much as a vitality of spirit. Lutfisk has soul.

At Day Fish as well as at other local proprietors, you'll need cash or checks to make a purchase, as no credit card machines or computers of any kind are available.

Lutfisk sales and credit cards don't mix. Maybe it's the honesty of the fish, but if you want to eat or purchase lutfisk from real people, bring real money or a checkbook.

Day Fish is a family business purchased by brothers Roy and Walt Bolling in 1968. The day we visited Day Fish, nephew David was running things, moving quickly to retrieve frozen sausage from the aged refrigerator, wrapping smoked fillets in brown butcher paper, and gruffly chuckling at the lutfisk jokes customers told—jokes he's likely heard repeated a hundred times each day from October to February his entire life. No one tells more jokes about lye fish than those of us who partake in it. Good-natured banter among customers makes the wait and the smell almost enjoyable.

Cases of rye crackers, lefse, lingonberry preserves, and pickled fish were stacked on a long table along the back wall of the shop. Above the table were a few hand-written signs listing ingredients and prices. David used a handheld calculator to ring up orders while handling cash, checks, and pickled herring with the ease of a man born to the task.

He invited us to the back of the store, sort of a stockroom meets mini-warehouse. An overhead light flickered (David mentioned he was meaning to get it fixed) over rows of vats holding cod in various stages of the lutfisking process. The cod arrives at Day Fish from Norway, flat and brittle, air-dried to the point of desiccation. The Bollings revive the fish in a tank of water before the saturated fillets soak in lye until they puff like sponges. After the lye, the cod goes back into a water tank to rinse off the lye. The entire process takes up to three weeks, and the result is a delicate fillet that, cooked properly, is almost as flaky as walleye fresh from the lake. (Cooked improperly, lutfisk becomes gelatinous sludge unfit for consumption let alone enjoyment.)

The uncomplicated prep secures each fillet with its holiday destiny in church basements, community kitchens, and the ovens of stalwart families. I moved between the tubs and filtering hoses, peering down at the chubby ribbons of floating white fish, and thought about the communion I feel when sitting at a table filled with strangers, eating lutfisk covered with melted butter and béchamel. We gravitate toward this communal meal not necessarily because of the flavors, although some of us do love the taste of lutfisk. We gather for the annual feast mostly because it reminds us of where we've been, or certainly where our grandparents and their grandparents came from. It is a humbling reminder, perfumed with allspice, a few boiled potatoes, and a pile of peas (for color).

My husband, unable to endure the odor, headed outdoors, where I found him chatting with a small group of other customers, still exchanging lutfisk jokes, and slipping in an occasional crack about Norwegians versus Swedes.

We packed ourselves and a few packages of lefse into the car, looked at one another, and immediately opened the windows to let the sleet drip in and the aroma leach out. A few miles into our ride home, my husband gave me a strange glance. "I think it's you. You are the smell."

It was true. My clothing, hair, skin: every bit of me reeked of a sardine can left open for a week in a dirty aquarium, as if I'd splashed for hours in the casks of reconstituted cod.

At home, we stripped down in the garage and took turns in the shower. I washed my hair twice and mentally abandoned plans to attend a lutfisk supper in Duluth a few weeks away.

Gradually, I forgot the smell. I think the process of making lutfisk is like the stories we hear about giving birth. During the experience, we might claim to never want to do it again. But afterward, we only recall the bliss that comes from the pain.

## 2. Fake it till you make it. But be sure to do your homework.

The marketing director at the American Swedish Institute included me on an email invitation to meet with the producers of a BBC Two show about American train travel. They were preparing to shoot season two, with an emphasis on immigration. From James J. Hill to our Scandinavian and European ancestors, Minnesota was a great place to start.

We gathered at ASI to talk about what the producers were looking for as they filmed in Minneapolis and St. Paul. As the food representative, I was soon answering questions about immigrant foodways and explaining that what we consider Swedish food in Minnesota is often very different from what modern Swedes eat. Our concept of Swedish food is informed by what our immigrant great-grandparents brought with them when they came here one hundred years ago, and is now mostly prepared and eaten by us during the holidays.

"Meatballs of course are the iconic Swedish dish," I offered, excited to deliver a rehearsed speech about my favorite food.

"And lutfisk!" added someone (who will not be named, but you know who you are).

"Lutfisk? What's that" asked a BBCer.

"Lutfisk is a fish, usually cod, that is dried, then soaked in lye, then soaked in water to rinse out the toxins." I watched the BBCers' faces light up. Someone else described the ritual of lutfisk church dinners, and I added that I knew a guy who runs a lutfisk locator website and keeps a small jar of allspice in his coat pocket in case someone serves him lutfisk without the seasoning.

"That sounds exactly like what our viewers would love to see!" The BBCers scribbled excitedly on their notepads and murmured, "Colorful! Wonderful! Strange!" They asked, "What does it taste like?"

Ever the lutfisk apologist, I answered, "It is more about the texture than the taste. It is sort of gelatinous, but if it is cooked well it can be almost flaky, like walleye."

"Wall . . . eye?" The BBCers looked confused.

"Walleye is a lake fish really popular in our region," someone explained.

Everyone in the room was getting lutfisk fever, and our conversation moved into planning a lutfisk dinner complete with musicians and distinguished guests. "Our host is this illustrious former politician, and we really enjoy putting him in silly situations. We could have him help you make the fish, then serve it."

One of the ASI staff turned to me and asked, "Do you bake or boil your lutfisk?"

Without hesitation I answered, "Oh, steaming is the only proper way to cook lutfisk." It felt like the right answer, provided by someone who, while having indulged in quite a few lutfisk dinners, had never actually prepared the delicacy in her own kitchen. Heck, I could figure it out. It's just fish. How hard could it be?

Lutfisk usually comes from the fishmonger frozen. I stood at the long glass counter that frames the back wall at Ingebretsen's Meat Market. I had called ahead to reserve a seven-pound chunk of iced lye fish, and the butcher gave me a stern look as he handed over the paper package. He warned, "It needs more time to thaw than you can imagine." I told him I was making the fish that Thursday. "Take it out of the freezer Monday morning. That should give you enough time."

Thursday afternoon I assembled the ingredients necessary to feed a dozen-plus lutfisk devotees. I rolled tiny meatballs and then quick-pickled beets and cucumbers. My kitchen buddy Chelsea buttered two dozen lefse triangles. We whisked together a roux for the cream and mustard sauce, melted butter with lemon, and added dill to the boiled potatoes and peas.

The lutfisk, still wrapped in butcher paper and thawing for four days, remained frozen in a lump. I jammed my fingers between the fillets and managed to separate them, then pressed the flesh with clean paper towels to release some of the crystallized liquid. I could see Chelsea's eyes searching mine for panic. I felt none. These fillets were going to finish thawing, and our dinner would be a success. I'd followed the butcher's instructions, and on this very important night, serving dinner to very important people for a very important network, fish failure was not an option.

Cooking lutfisk on TV didn't intimidate me, but cooking it for a table filled with Scandinavian food experts was terrifying. We'd even invited Jim Norris, the lutfisk lover who runs that website providing locations and times for lutfisking around the country (http://lutfiskloverslifeline.com/). I especially didn't want to let Jim down. He's the guy who taught me to always bring my own jar of allspice. These guests would sense any mistake, be it overcooked peas or undercooked fish. Earlier, I'd practiced making the gooey fish. Relying on my presumed ability to improvise any recipe, I'd kept the lutfisk in the oven three or four minutes past Scandinavian and Finnish cookbook author Beatrice Ojakangas's instructions. One moment the fish was plump and intact, and a second later it was deflated sludge, steamy and oozing.

I armed myself with Beatrice's lutfisk knowledge, the assurance that comes from meticulous planning, and a will to have some fun. While my nerves were still high, there was a moment or two of serenity as I slipped the (finally) thawed fish into a buttered dish and confidently guided the BBC host as he sprinkled white pepper and allspice over flabby white fillets.

Dinner was a success! We dined in style out on the lawn under warm summer skies. There were folk songs and drinking songs and plenty of aquavit. And there was no lutfisk left over.

### 3. Not everyone agrees with your opinion, but you cannot argue with science.

Unless you are making pasta, rice, or dumplings, there is almost always a better cooking method than boiling. Sure, there are plenty of lutfisk lovers who argue that boiling is best. Do not listen to them. If you decide to boil the lutfisk, don't drain it in the sink. It may slither down the drain like a runaway octopus. And while I am not exactly sure what the exact science behind boiling lutfisk is, the best option is to NEVER boil the lutfisk.

On the other hand, the same people who boil their lye fish might also pronounce it with an additional vowel. Not everyone pronounces words the same. And that's okay. *Lutfisk* is the proper Swedish spelling and is pronounced loot-fisk. The more common Norwegian spelling is *lutefisk* and is pronounced loot-ah-fisk. The exact interpretation is lye fish. In this text the Swedish spelling is used when referring to Swedish foodways, and the Norwegian spelling is used when it is within a quote or when referring to Norwegian foodways.

### 4. Honor your heritage. Live in the moment while you celebrate the past. Let someone else take photos.

"Hey you old Norskey!" A gruff man's voice greeted the woman standing in line behind me.

"Hey Bill, are you still going to sing at my funeral?"

"Well, you haven't given me the date yet so I haven't got it on my calendar." The two friends laughed and hugged, then started talking about who was and wasn't joining them for the annual lutfisk and meatball lunch at First Lutheran Church in Columbia Heights, Minnesota. The meal, set for mid-January, is one of the last in the season; most lutfisk dinners happen between Thanksgiving and Christmas.

"Oh, Helen couldn't make it. She fell again."

Around me I heard snippets of conversation rise above the murmur of voices. In front and behind me, everyone seemed to be exchanging dates and locations for the best places they had enjoyed lutfisk earlier in the season. After Bill walked away, funeral lady gently touched my arm and told me I had a white thread on my skirt. Would I mind if she removed it? She immediately patted my tush and apologized for her forwardness. This is a Minnesota thing. We are shy enough to ask for permission but don't hesitate to help someone in need. We began a conversation about good places to go for lutfisk. Funeral lady confided, "Oh, they've got a good one on Fridays in December over at Mindekirken . . . and Jax has one, too! They got one at Jax! And we had some at the VFW last year. Real good."

Something people outside of the Midwest don't understand is our accents. If you aren't from around here, you might believe that the characters in the movie and spin-off television show *Fargo* speak with the defining regional accent. They do not. In fact, our accents are so complex and beautiful that many of us locals can distinguish someone from northeast Minneapolis, east St. Paul, and Gaylord, Minnesota, with the first two sentences of a conversation, sort of like that old game show *Name That Tune*: "I can name that accent in seven syllables."

There is a lilt and lingering cadence to the relaxed yet suffer-no-fools speech of the old-timers hailing from northeast Minneapolis. I am drawn to it, this drawl influenced by a few dozen countries and many thousands of immigrants who made this place home a hundred-plus years ago. It is the song of my people. There is a beauty to its economy:

"So you guys came all the way from Zimmerman?"

"Yah. Not too bad of a drive today. Pretty clear."

"You been to this church before?"

"Nope. You?"

Outside the main church entrance, a short line of cars dropped off the elderly. I watched the parade of walkers, canes, wheelchairs, and the occasional lady clinging to the arm of a loved one gently guiding her up the slick sidewalk to the wide glass entrance. Inside the church, hundreds gathered in the lobby and found seats in pews within the sanctuary. An expanse of coatracks groaned from the weight of fluffy down coats and heavy wool jackets.

We able-bodied stood in line to pick up our meal tickets, most already paid for with checks we mailed in prior to the event. For about twenty dollars we were about to receive all the lutfisk we could possibly swallow, served with butter and white sauce, meatballs, mashed potatoes, mashed rutabaga, pickled beets and herring, lefse, *julkake*, carrots, coleslaw, rice pudding, and ginger cookies. Our tickets were marked in black ink with a number from one to two hundred, noting our place in line. Mine said 189.

I took my ticket, hung my coat, and found a seat in the pews where I could observe the crowd. The ratio of Norwegian sweaters to other forms of dress: 2:1. The ratio of people over eighty years old to those under: 4:1. White people to people of color: 40:1, and most of the people of color were children and church volunteers.

There was a jovial feel to the festivities as we waited for the hostess to begin calling out numbers so we could take our places in the food line. I inhaled the familiar church smell of leather, aftershave, and the holy water that filled an enormous baptismal fountain in the back of the church.

The intercom squealed and a hush went over the crowd. "Testing. Testing. Welcome to . . . testing. *Screeeeeeeech*." Then there was a pause followed by chuckles from hungry diners. "Guests with ticket numbers one through ten, please start lining up."

The guys behind me joked, "We got a long ways to go if they're only doing ten at a time." There was a bingo hall quality to the scene, and we waited anxiously to win the raffle.

"Eleven through twenty-seven!"

At the altar I noticed a cloth sign with the phrase, "I have called you by name. You are mine." I read it silently as "I have called your number. Get in line."

I leaned sideways in my pew to eavesdrop on the guys behind me. "I don't need no potatoes. I got burned out on boiled potatoes growing up. Just give me the lutfisk and the meatballs. And some lefse."

I heard the other guy smack his lips in agreement, "Oh, I love lefse. How can I describe it? So soft."

As the hostess called numbers, entire pews of people rose and rushed to stand in the food line, our third line of the day. Minnesotans are patient line standers. It is where we develop our ability to small talk, especially about non-controversial topics like the weather.

My number was finally called, and I found myself in line with the same family I waited with in the first line. The youngish son chaperoned his mom, grandma, and grandma's friend to the lunch. He confided that they also love Friday night fish fries, which would begin in just a few weeks as the promise of spring ushers in Lent.

Two food lines formed on either side of the large kitchen window. Inside the kitchen, volunteers scrambled to put out huge foil baking tins of lutfisk and crocks filled with meatballs and carrots. Everyone was in high spirits. The guy with the lutfisk spoon, ready to lift the wiggly fish onto my plate, rolled his eyes at my request for a card deck–sized fillet, considered a tiny portion, which the woman with the meatballs made up for by giving me three rather than two. I teetered through the potato, rutabaga, coleslaw, and sauce line with a dangerously overflowing plate. The walk to find my assigned table was equally precarious, and I wove to avoid walkers and a small child dancing in the aisles.

"Room for one more?" I asked brightly when I found a lone place at a full table. Seven mostly elderly faces stared up at me with Minnesota niceness that gradually became camaraderie. (Minnesota nice is our way of pretending not to be uncomfortable around people we haven't known long enough to talk about behind their backs.)

Around us, the room bustled with child and adult volunteers hoofing pickled beets and hot coffee to tables and busing away the empties. A woman with a plate filled with *julkaka* used plastic tongs to nestle a slice of the sweet bread at the edge of my rutabaga. Someone asked if I wanted milk, and I saw that half of my tablemates had small cartons, the kind we drank from in elementary school, next to their meals. The lefse basket made its rounds, and I took my time spreading thick layers of butter on a soft piece of potato bread, then tucked it next to slivers of pickled herring.

After a deep appreciative sigh of admiration for the masterpiece before me, I dug in.

The perfect lutfisk plate is a mix of flavors, colors, temperatures, and textures. It is a thing of beauty and enormity. As many times as I've tried, I've never been able to finish a plate at lutfisk dinner. All around me, tiny ninety-pound women eat like they've never been fed before: ravenous, greedy, asking for seconds, and sneaking cod fillets into Baggie-lined purses. Clean plate club jokes are aimed at me, and in disgrace I always end up handing my half-full plate to a kid clearing dishes.

"Do I still get rice pudding if I don't finish my meal?" I asked, knowing my peripheral Pink Floyd reference would be lost on pretty much everyone within earshot. The little girl tending our table glared at me, and I felt that I dishonored the entire room.

Soon enough a cup of hot coffee and a dish of cold pudding were placed in front of me, and I couldn't finish those, either.

A word about church coffee. Church coffee in the northern states has a universal flavor and temperature. It doesn't taste like Starbucks. It tastes like the stuff my great-aunt Hazel brewed: a combination of dirt, hot water, and some undefinable muddle. It is steeped in pots seasoned with thousands of Sunday sermons, funerals and celebrations, and the dust of pure souls. When poured into an empty cup it is hot enough to burn your mouth, but within seconds it becomes too cold for consumption.

My tablemates began to tell me their stories. That is probably the best part of any lutfisk meal: hearing the stories of strangers. The stories, like the coffee and overflowing plates, are familiar and comforting. "My mom made lutfisk every year. I grew up eating it. And I love it."

"I wonder which fish place they get the lutfisk from," I said. "And how much do they make? And how many meatballs?"

One of my dining companions reached for a small stack of leaflets in the middle of the table. "Maybe this will answer your questions," he said, handing me a blue paper with the title "Did You Know."

I started reading the facts out loud. "Wow! Two hundred fifty-six guests times three meals! A thousand pounds of lutfisk! Three thousand meatballs! Seventy pounds of herring! Hey! This lutfisk comes from Day Fish! I went there this fall!"

My tablemates feigned interest in my The More You Know moment, and soon our meal was over.

After lunch I waited in the church lobby for Harriet and John "Forrest" Anderson. Longtime church members and lutfisk aficionados, Harriet and John moved through the crowd slowly as friends greeted them and stopped to chat. John told me that any young folks in the lutfisk line probably weren't there willingly. "You won't see anybody under fifty. It might be that somebody really loves their grandmother, and there are kids helping serve. We jokingly speak of this as the Holy High Feast of Lutfisk."

Like most of the over-fifty guests, Harriet and Forrest grew up eating lutfisk. "My grandmother boiled it. It turned out like jelly. It was still edible." Forrest hesitated, then added, "But after three generations and four methods of preparation, baking is by far the best of the bunch. My mother simply steamed it. Now that was better: flakey. By the time Harriet and I made it, we baked or microwaved it."

Harriet attended St. Olaf College for nursing. Her Norwegian parents spoke Norwegian when they didn't want Harriet and her siblings to understand what they were talking about. "My mother would never teach me Norwegian, so I took Spanish at St. Olaf. When I was at St. Olaf I remember standing in line at the old dining hall to eat at the lutefisk dinner. I learned the importance of being Norwegian. My parents were less concerned about being Norwegian and more concerned about being Americans."

Of Christmases past, Harriet joked, "My grandpa always had to have oyster stew. Now, if someone is going to eat the oysters, it is Forrest. I eat them only under duress." Harriet described her family's typical Christmas meal: "We have a varied menu at Christmas. I buy good meatballs from the grocery store." Because their children have never been fans of lutfisk, Harriet usually makes the cod in the days following Christmas dinner.

Forrest pulled a small jar out of his pocket. "I bring dry mustard. I am specialized to mustard." I told him I'd learned the trick of bringing my own allspice to lutfisk meals but had never seen mustard before, and I made a note to try it on my next fillet.

## 5. Camouflage and clean up should happen immediately.

Everyone who loves lutfisk knows that when you are introducing the experience to a newcomer, it is best to follow the rules of CAMOUFLAGE: Cute Accessories Make the Outfit (Fish Liberates a Gelatinous Explosion). In other words, be generous with the cream and butter: they hide a multitude of sins. Bring your own allspice (or dry mustard!), and be willing to share the jar.

My mom tells a great story about the first time she ate Christmas Eve dinner with my dad's Swedish family. My aunties served lutfisk before the main meal, with plenty of cream sauce and butter. "I didn't have time to taste the fish! It just slid down my throat!" My mom laughs at the memory and always adds that she liked lutfisk; it is just fish, after all.

What always strikes me about Mom's story is that she recalls she had barely finished eating her fish before the aunties raced around the table collecting the good silver so it could soak in warm, soapy water. "They didn't want the silver to tarnish."

What on earth is in the lutfisk that could tarnish silver?

Soaking the cookware and serving dishes is also important, but for a different reason. Once lutfisk cools it becomes a fish cement, impossible to remove from any surface it adheres to.

## 6. There is no bad lutfisk, only bad cooks.
There is a saying that speaks to a Scandinavian's soul: There is no such thing as bad weather, only bad clothes. The same is true of lutfisk. Keep an open mind, and enjoy the season.

# Lutfisk

Lutfisk is typically stored frozen in two- to three-pound packages. Be sure to purchase the fish well in advance and plan on leaving several days for the fish to thaw completely. Keep fish in packaging and thaw in the refrigerator for about one day per pound of fish.

⤛ ⤜

6 pounds ready-to-cook lutfisk, thawed

3 teaspoons salt

½ teaspoon white pepper

½ teaspoon allspice

3 tablespoons butter, cut into teaspoons

Preheat oven to 350 degrees. Remove as much residual liquid as possible from fish by pressing flesh with paper towels, using fresh towels as needed. Place fish in generously buttered baking dish. (If lutfisk comes with skin, place skin side down.) Season with salt, pepper, and allspice. Dot surface with butter. Cover baking dish with foil and bake for 35 minutes. Do not overcook or fish will turn to sludge. Drain liquid from baking dish. Fish should flake but still appear slightly gelatinous. Slice fish into serving sizes and serve in clean dish, with béchamel and butter sauce.

**For the béchamel**

3 tablespoons butter

3 tablespoons flour

2 ½–3 cups half-and-half

1 teaspoon salt

½ teaspoon white pepper

1–2 tablespoons coarse-ground mustard (or your favorite mustard, but do not use sweet)

nutmeg

In saucepan, melt butter over medium-high heat; whisk in flour. Continue to whisk roux, cooking until it begins to thicken and loses its floury taste. Stir in half-and-half and increase heat to high. Continue whisking until mixture thickens. Remove from heat and whisk in salt, pepper, and mustard. Season to taste with a bit of nutmeg. Serve hot in gravy boat with spoon.

**For the butter sauce**

1 cup (2 sticks) butter

¼ cup hot water

juice of 1 lemon

salt

In saucepan over low heat, melt butter. Whisk in water and lemon juice; season to taste with salt. Serve hot in gravy boat with spoon.

SERVES 6–20, DEPENDING ON
HOW MUCH THEY LOVE IT

# Baked Cod

When Swedish chef Magnus Nilsson visited Minnesota in 2016, he wondered at our collective reach toward lutfisk. When beautiful fresh cod is available, why would anyone eat lutfisk? If you are unwilling to try the lye fish, baked cod is a perfectly acceptable and delicious substitute.

½ cup flour

1 tablespoon dry mustard

1 tablespoon paprika

zest and juice of 1 lemon

1 teaspoon salt

1 teaspoon pepper

1 ½ pounds cod

½ cup (1 stick) butter, melted

½ teaspoon ground nutmeg

Preheat oven to 450 degrees. In shallow dish, whisk together flour, mustard, paprika, zest, salt, and pepper. Dredge cod in flour mixture to coat all sides. Place cod in baking dish and pour butter over fillet. Sprinkle with nutmeg. Bake uncovered for 12 to 15 minutes or until cod flakes. Sprinkle lemon juice over entire dish and serve immediately.

**SERVES 4**

# Peas

2 teaspoons sugar

3 cups frozen peas

3 tablespoons butter

1–2 tablespoons fresh dill

1–2 tablespoons fresh chives

salt and pepper

In large pot, bring ½ cup water to boil. Add sugar and peas. Cook until peas are just thawed, about 3 minutes. Remove from heat and stir in butter and herbs. Season to taste with salt and pepper. Serve immediately.

SERVES 4

# Potato Puree

3–4 pounds Yukon gold potatoes, peeled and quartered

¼ cup (½ stick) butter

about 1 cup heavy cream

salt and pepper

Add potatoes to a large pot of heavily salted water and bring to boil. Cook, uncovered, until potatoes are fork tender. Drain potatoes and push through a ricer. Return pot to low heat and add butter and as much cream as you like. When butter is melted, gently stir in potatoes and season to taste with salt and pepper.

SERVES 4

# White Sauce — all purpose AND for lutefisk!

**Gustavus Adolphus College, St. Peter, Minnesota**

"Some swear by melted butter alone, some swear by white sauce alone, some swear by some of each and plenty of salt and pepper to accompany their Christmas lutefisk. Whatever your pleasure, this white sauce has many uses, and if our guests wish to bathe this gelatinous 'delicacy' in it, we are pleased to offer it!"

3 tablespoons butter

3 tablespoons flour

3 cups heavy cream (or use half-and-half for a lighter sauce)

salt and white pepper

In heavy saucepan, melt butter and add flour. Whisk to combine; cook roux for 2 minutes. Whisk in cream, 1 cup at a time, and heat to simmer. Season to taste with salt and pepper.

SERVES 12

# four

## MEATBALLS
## & RICE PUDDING

# *No single dish*

is more evocative of Swedish *jul* than the humble meatball. How did the meatball become the icon of Swedish dining?

Swedish meatballs are linked to exiled Swedish king Charles XII. It is believed that he brought the notion of meatballs with him when he returned from Istanbul in 1713, as meatballs have long been essential Middle Eastern fare in many forms (such as kebab and kofta). The first Swedish meatball recipe appeared in print in the mid-1750s when famous cook and author Cajsa Warg wrote about them in her wildly successful *Hjelpreda I Hushållningen För Unga Fruentimber* (Guide to Housekeeping for Young Women).

Considered a peasant food in many cultures, the meatball stretches small amounts of meat into large meals. However, meatballs (*köttbullar*) in Sweden utilized the luxury ingredients beef, veal, and pork, making them highly popular among royalty and peasants alike. Eventually they appeared on celebratory buffets and *smörgåsbord*, where they now reign as an iconic Swedish dish.

Swedish immigrants brought their beloved meatball with them to the United States, where the dish became common especially in the northern Midwest. In the 1950s and '60s, nationwide acceptance transformed the Swedish meatball into fancy cocktail and dinner party fare.

While the American Swedish meatball mostly exists in a taste vacuum, some regional changes occurred. My Swedish friends find it humorous that many Americans serve their meatballs covered in gravy and over noodles. A real Swede would never allow such culinary travesties.

In modern Sweden, meatballs underwent changes, as do foodways everywhere. In some recipes, Italian seasonings replaced allspice and garlic replaced onion. One characteristic that did not change, however, was the belief that "Mom's meatball is always best." Meatballs are common to most cultures, and that mantra seems to be accurate regardless of where the meatball is prepared.

During Christmas, the Swedish meatball rarely appears without its most important companions: potatoes (either boiled or pureed), pickled cucumbers, and lingonberry preserves. Cream sauce (white gravy) or brown sauce (brown gravy) also may be on offer.

Christmas Eve in my house has always been Feast of the Meatball. For one hundred years, possibly longer, someone in my family has stood over the meatballs, making sure each little orb is seared in hot butter to seal in the goodness of ground meat, allspice, mustard, cream, and soft bread. For one hundred years, possibly longer, someone in my family understood the importance of serving her (or his) family the traditional Christmas Eve meal. Making the meatballs is a rite of passage.

When my parents divorced, my dad had us sisters on Christmas Eve. He took over the meatball duties. There were two techniques my dad always applied to his cooking: fry everything in butter, and cook meat until it is done (and then cook it some more). Dad's dry, burned meatballs remain a memory that tasted like the end of childhood innocence. But they are also the taste of my sisters and me when we were still together during the holidays, before we separated and moved on and away from one another.

In the years when my daughter was a vegetarian, I'd make a batch of veggie balls and a batch of regular. Later, when she ate chicken, I made chicken balls; then she started eating bison, and we had bison balls. There are more delicious versions of Swedish meatballs than you can shake a skillet at, even just in our home.

I've enjoyed Swedish meatballs at some of the fanciest restaurants in our city. I've had meatballs in church basements, served alongside lutfisk and lefse. I've even had more than my fair share of those prefabricated, colorless balls from a certain blue and yellow big box store known for its flat boxes of furniture that needs assembling. I consider myself a meatball historian and connoisseur.

While Mom's meatballs are always best, I think my dad's burned meatballs are the ones I miss the most.

The American Swedish Institute in Minneapolis, Minnesota, was preparing for a makeover: an expansion of the museum.

Those of us who feel at home in the mansion—or the castle, as many of us call her—on Park Avenue were intrigued with the expansion chatter, but we were also steeling ourselves for the semi-closure of our beloved museum. During construction, many of the events we'd come to expect would be curtailed and rain-checked for post-construction festivities.

To ease our worries, ASI threw a construction kickoff party in the mansion that included a meatball contest, with three finalists vying for top ball bragging rights in three categories: People's Choice, Kids' Choice, and Overall.

There is a saying across cultures that Mom's meatball is the best. This is true of Swedish meatballs as well, although some diners prefer Grandma's meatballs, or Dad's. At the meatball competition, Faye Olson's meatballs were best. Never throw your meatball in the ring against a professional.

# Swedish Meatballs

Faye Olson, Brooklyn Park, Minnesota

"This recipe won People's Choice and Kids' Choice Awards at the American Swedish Institute contest in 2011."

1 cup bread crumbs

1 ½ teaspoons salt

⅓ teaspoon pepper

1 ½ teaspoons seasoned salt

2 teaspoons onion powder

¾ cup half-and-half

2 eggs

dash allspice (optional)

2 ½ pounds ground beef

Preheat oven to 375 degrees. In large mixing bowl, thoroughly combine all ingredients except beef; set aside until mixture resembles oatmeal, about 5 minutes. Mix in beef until well combined. Shape into walnut-sized balls and place on parchment-lined baking sheets with at least 1-inch-high sides. Bake for 10 to 15 minutes.

**MAKES ABOUT 42 MEATBALLS**

# My Swedish Meatballs

Susan Swanson, Mahtowa, Minnesota

"Adapted from my mom and grandma's recipe. My spice additions
   are nutmeg and more pepper."

1 pound lean ground beef

8 ounces lean ground pork

½ cup minced onion

¾ cup soft bread crumbs

1 ½ teaspoons salt

½ teaspoon pepper

1 teaspoon freshly grated nutmeg

1 egg, beaten

½ cup milk

1–2 (14 ½–ounce) cans beef broth

Combine beef, pork, onion, bread crumbs, salt, pepper, nutmeg, and egg and mix well. Add milk and mix; chill overnight.

Preheat oven to 350 degrees. Shape mixture into balls and place in a cake pan or on a baking sheet with at least 1-inch sides. Bake until meatballs turn a deep caramel brown color, about 30 minutes. Remove meatballs from baking pan and put into a casserole dish or slow cooker. Add beef broth and continue cooking at 275 degrees or on the slow cooker's low setting. Add more nutmeg, salt, and pepper to taste. The meatballs are done when you like the taste, approximately 30 minutes in the oven or up to several hours in the slow cooker.

SERVES 6

# Swedish Meatballs

Gustavus Adolphus College, St. Peter, Minnesota

"Whatever the season, there's always a reason for Swedish Meatballs! The warmth of home and hospitality come front and center with the first bite and each bite after. Serve with Swedish Meatball Sauce (page 125), brown gravy, or even a creamy white sauce."

½ cup chopped onion

1 ½ pounds ground beef

12 ounces ground pork

1 ½ cups dried, finely ground bread crumbs

3 eggs

¼ cup sugar

1 teaspoon salt

1 teaspoon ground nutmeg

1 teaspoon pepper

¾ cup 2 percent milk

Preheat oven to 350 degrees. Cook onions in heavy skillet in a little olive oil or butter, stirring occasionally, until soft and translucent. Add all ingredients, including onion, to a large mixing bowl and mix to combine but do not overmix. Hand roll or scoop into 1 ½–inch meatballs and place on a parchment-lined baking pan. Bake until a thermometer reads 160 degrees and centers are no longer pink, 35 to 40 minutes.

**MAKES 12 SERVINGS OF 3 MEATBALLS EACH**

# Swedish Meatball Sauce

Gustavus Adolphus College, St. Peter, Minnesota

"There are many versions of sauce for Swedish Meatballs, and this is one of them. The nutmeg and lemon juice are subtle and add a depth that makes our customers want to eat this sauce by the bowlful."

2 tablespoons butter

2 tablespoons flour

2 cups heavy cream (or use half-and-half for a lighter version)

2 tablespoons concentrated beef broth base

⅛ teaspoon freshly grated nutmeg

2 teaspoons lemon juice concentrate

1 cup sour cream

salt and white pepper

Melt butter in heavy saucepan and stir in flour to form a roux. Slowly whisk heavy cream into roux and heat to simmer. Mix beef base with a little warm water to dissolve and add to sauce. Add nutmeg and lemon juice and return to simmer over low heat, stirring occasionally. Whisk in sour cream and return to simmer. If too thick, stir in a little milk or half-and-half. Season to taste with salt and white pepper.

SERVES 12

# *Kristine*
## BOLANDER

My family are Swedish, but not all that Swedish: the only Swedish things about us were the name, the looks, and the jar of pickled herring in the refrigerator. Otherwise, although my grandfather immigrated when he was a teenager, we did not ever do anything particularly Swedish. Until Christmas.

Every year, my grandparents took us to the American Swedish Institute [in Minneapolis, Minnesota] at Christmas. We had the straw goat, the angel candles, the orange horse. When my grandparents became too old and unwell to take us to ASI, we quit going. My sister and I were the only ones who were included on this excursion: I think my grandmother secretly hoped we would consent to be Lucia one year, but there was no way either of us were going to agree to putting candles anywhere near our hair.

The food at Christmas Eve dinner was really our principal connection with our Swedish heritage. When I was young, every Christmas Eve we would gather at my grandparents' house. We were allowed to open all the presents from Grandma and Grandpa that night, so that was one of the big draws. Then we would have dinner, and every year, the same two dishes would feature: Swedish meatballs and rice pudding (from my grandfather's mother's recipes). When cooking the Christmas Eve dinner got to be too much for my grandmother, my mother took it over, which meant that we were all charged with making the meatballs and the rice pudding as soon as we were old enough to hold a spoon.

The recipes are unusual, and a bit labor intensive by today's standards. The meatballs were hand mixed and hand formed and were meant to

be the size of walnuts: this was important, because there was a yearly competition between my two brothers as to how many meatballs they could eat at Christmas Eve dinner. The record was held by my father, and the number was thirty-eight or something ridiculous like that. I think my brother Richard may have beaten that number once.

When my mother and my sister and I took over making the meatballs, they got larger, like golf balls, sometimes even larger; nobody was eating thirty meatballs anymore. There was one year, when my mother's dementia had progressed from bad to awful and my father's health was also not good, my sister-in-law and I made the meatballs. There was so much going on, with the grandparents needing attention and the grandkids running around, we were really not into making the meatballs. We made them too big, and under-fried them, and we served them undercooked. Nobody really ate meatballs that year; they were pretty awful.

My grandparents died years ago; my parents have both passed on more recently. My sister does not make the meatballs anymore. I do not make them because my son thinks they are too dry; he did not realize that Swedish meatballs usually have sauce on them until the first time he went to IKEA. Now that is how he likes them. My brother Richard still serves them for his family every year, and when I join them for Christmas Eve, I eat them, too. Last year, my brother made the meatballs and the rice pudding, and my sister-in-law, who is Thai, made a lot of delicious Thai food. It was a pretty eclectic menu.

The rice pudding is an unusual recipe as well. It is not sweet, and not all that creamy, and it is not meant to be a dessert. It is a side dish. Out of

my family, I think I am the only one who actually likes it. We still make it every year even though it is a bit of a pain to make: the rice has to be stirred with milk for hours, then whipped egg whites folded in, then it has to bake. My sister claims that every year she refused it, and every year my dad asked her, "Since when do you not like rice pudding?" and every year she replied, "Since always." Needless to say, Susan does not make the rice pudding ever. I do not make it because I prefer the dessert kind of rice pudding, preferably made with coconut milk. The only common element is cardamom: whenever I smell cardamom, I think of Christmas at my grandparents' house when I was small. The only time I eat the family rice pudding recipe is at my brother Richard's house, where he and his wife carry on the tradition for another generation.

In the end it is not about whether these are good recipes or not; it is about the whole family in the kitchen, stirring the rice in milk or frying the meatballs. It is remembering the year we could not find cinnamon zwieback or whole cardamom and had to improvise. It is, like many family recipes, much more about family than the recipe.

My sister-in-law is an outstanding cook, and she has been making the meatballs and pudding for my brother and nieces every year. I have included her meatball recipe. This is a recipe from her Shan heritage and has proven very popular at potlucks and school fundraisers. It has little in common with the Swedish meatballs, but it comes from her family and I thought it was interesting.

The whole thing started with one Swede, my grandfather, and has been carried on by non-Swedes and quarter-Swedes since.

# Swedish Meatballs

Kristine Bolander, the Bolander Family, in memory of Dorothy, David, Alice, and Ivar, with special thanks to Mae Bolander, Minneapolis, Minnesota

I was unable to find zwieback toast, but Carla Grant Adams provided her family's rusk recipe (page 82), and it makes a wonderful substitute. Use 1 to 1 ¼ cups of toasted crumbs.

5 pounds lean ground pork

4 cinnamon zwieback toasts, crushed

1 medium onion, minced

approximately 1 cup heavy cream

2 teaspoons salt

½ teaspoon pepper

2 eggs

Combine all ingredients and make into balls about the size of walnuts. Heat some oil in a skillet and fry meatballs slowly in batches until cooked through. May be removed from the fire when not quite done and finished, covered, in a 300-degree oven.

**MAKES 168 MEATBALLS**

# Shan Meatballs

Kristine Bolander, the Bolander Family, in memory of Dorothy, David, Alice, and Ivar, with special thanks to Mae Bolander, Minneapolis, Minnesota

Serve with sticky rice.

3 pounds ground pork

2 tablespoons ginger paste
or grated fresh ginger

1 tablespoon garlic paste or chopped garlic

1 tablespoon plus 1 teaspoon
chopped shallots

5 medium tomatoes, chopped

salt to taste

1 teaspoon turmeric

2 cups chopped green onions

2 cups chopped cilantro

Mix all ingredients in a big bowl and make into meatballs. In a wok, heat a little oil and, working in batches, add meatballs. Cook over medium heat. The juice in the tomatoes will come out; cook meatballs until dry and medium brown.

**MAKES 60 MEATBALLS**

# Swedish Meatballs

From Inga Rude Olson, contributed by her granddaughter, Kathy Weck, Farmington, Minnesota

"The recipe is supposed to make six servings. I usually triple it. I was generous with the spices and the dillweed as well. I also used half fat-free half-and-half to cut calories somewhat."

**For the meatballs**

2 eggs, slightly beaten

1 cup milk

½ cup dried bread crumbs

3 tablespoons butter

½ cup finely chopped onion

1 pound ground beef

4 ounces ground pork

1 ½ teaspoons salt

¼ teaspoon dried dill

¼ teaspoon ground allspice

⅛ teaspoon ground nutmeg

⅛ teaspoon ground cardamom

**For the sauce**

3 tablespoons flour

½ teaspoon salt

⅛ teaspoon pepper

1 (10 ½–ounce) can condensed beef broth

½ cup half-and-half

½ teaspoon dried dill

In a large bowl, combine eggs, milk, and bread crumbs. In a large skillet, heat 1 tablespoon butter. Cook onion, stirring often, until soft, about 5 minutes. Use a slotted spoon to remove onion from pan. Add to bread crumb mixture along with ground beef and ground pork, 1 ½ teaspoons salt, ¼ teaspoon dill, allspice, nutmeg, and cardamom. With wooden spoon or your hands, mix well to combine. Refrigerate, covered, for 1 hour.

Shape meat mixture into meatballs, about 1 inch in diameter. Add 1 tablespoon butter to large skillet over medium-high heat and cook meatballs in small batches until browned all over, adding more butter as needed. Remove the meatballs to a buttered 2-quart casserole.

Preheat oven to 325 degrees. Remove skillet from heat and reserve 2 tablespoons drippings, adding more butter if necessary. Whisk in flour, ½ teaspoon salt, and the pepper, stirring until smooth. Gradually whisk in beef broth; bring mixture to boil, stirring constantly. Stir in cream and ½ teaspoon dill. Pour over meatballs in casserole. Bake, covered, 30 minutes.

SERVES 6

# Swedish Meatballs and Gravy

Nancy Anderson, Cambridge, Minnesota

"There are many versions of Swedish meatballs, but this is mine."

1 ½ cups milk

3 eggs

1 teaspoon salt

1 sleeve saltine crackers, processed into fine crumbs

2 teaspoons brown sugar

½ teaspoon pepper

½ teaspoon ground nutmeg

½ teaspoon ground allspice

1 pound sausage

4 pounds ground beef

¼ cup (½ stick) butter

¼ cup flour

2 (14 ½–ounce) cans beef broth

1 cup half-and-half

Preheat oven to 400 degrees. Mix together milk, eggs, salt, cracker crumbs, brown sugar, and spices. Add the sausage and mix, then add the beef. Mix well with hands and form into small balls. Bake until browned and cooked through, about 20 minutes.

For gravy, in a saucepan, melt butter and stir in flour, then add broth and half-and-half. Bring to a boil and cook 2 minutes. Transfer baked meatballs to baking dish and pour gravy over. Reduce oven temperature to 350 degrees and bake for 30 to 45 minutes.

**MAKES ABOUT 170 BALLS**

When I was researching my master's thesis, I studied more than fifty Swedish meatball recipes. There were slight variances, such as how the onion was treated (sautéed, raw, grated, powdered) and whether mustard was added. Most included cream-soaked bread and allspice. Some included the fascinating addition of mashed potatoes.

Recipes change over time, influenced by an endless number of factors: travel, health, politics, immigration, wealth. When I developed this Modern Swedish Meatball recipe (page 134), I was thinking a lot about the changing face of Sweden, where, as in America, immigrants are an important part of culture. Sweden is no longer a pale, blonde, blue-eyed nation. It never really was. Culture is all about perception. Nothing made this clearer to me than when Aquavit, a Swedish restaurant in New York City with branches in Tokyo and Stockholm, landed briefly in Minneapolis.

Aquavit Minneapolis served evolving Scandinavian cuisine to diners, many, like me, who misunderstood the concept. At Aquavit, no chef stammered "Bork bork bork!" and no kitchen explosions penetrated the dining space. The modern interior was sleek and stylish, promoting the very best Scandinavian designs. Aquavit served ethereal feasts that imploded any preconceptions of Swedish cuisine. From tiny herring tacos served neat atop taro root shells to artful islands of coconut-lime rice pudding surrounded by a lake of citrus broth, the meals showcased Nordic ingredients (seafood, fish, game, seasonal produce) and cooking techniques (pickled, preserved) fused with nouvelle cuisine. Although, Swedish meatballs served with lingonberries, quick-cured cucumbers, and mashed potatoes also graced the menu.

Yet the most surprising thing I learned from Aquavit was that their renowned chef Marcus Samuelsson was the new face of Swedish food, and it wasn't pale. Samuelsson was born in Ethiopia and raised in Sweden by his adopted family. Now an American citizen living in Harlem, New York, Samuelsson continues to represent Sweden's progressive and evolving population.

I wanted my modern Swedish meatballs to include the best of the old and the best of the new. I add potatoes because they give meatballs a lovely soft texture. I grate the onion for flavor without a harsh bite. I include traditional allspice with an upgrade of oranges and nutmeg, flavors many of us associate with Swedish food, although they are imported from far outside the region. Panko bread crumbs, fresh ginger, and Sriracha represent the new immigrants of both Sweden and America, a nod to their contributions to our food world.

Swedish Meatballs

# Modern **Swedish Meatballs**
## with Lingonberry Reduction

Overall Best Meatball Award 2011, American Swedish Institute

**For the meatballs**

scant ⅔ cup panko bread crumbs

½ cup half-and-half

1 cup cooked russet potato, peeled, pushed through ricer, and cooled (about 1 potato)

1 medium yellow onion, grated (about ½ cup)

2 egg yolks

1 tablespoon prepared yellow or whole-grain mustard

1 ½ teaspoons grated fresh ginger (or ½ teaspoon ground)

1 teaspoon brown sugar

1 teaspoon salt

½ teaspoon pepper

½ teaspoon allspice

¼ teaspoon ground nutmeg

1 pound 85–90 percent lean ground beef

8 ounces ground pork

Preheat oven to 375 degrees; grease cake pans. Combine bread crumbs and half-and-half in medium bowl, stirring with spatula until crumbs are moistened and soak up half-and-half; stir in potato and set aside.

In a very large bowl mix onion, egg yolks, mustard, ginger, brown sugar, salt, pepper, allspice, and nutmeg; use your hands to combine thoroughly. Add beef and pork and mix well but gently. Add the bread crumb and half-and-half mixture and mix well.

With wet hands, shape tiny meatballs of a heaping tablespoon each. Place meatballs in prepared cake pans. Bake for

10 minutes; flip balls and continue cooking until internal temperature reads 160 degrees, about 15 minutes more. Meanwhile, prepare the reduction.

**For the reduction**

1 tablespoon butter

1 small shallot, chopped fine

¾ cup quality lingonberry preserves (Hafi or Felix)

½ cup dry red wine (Malbec or Pinot Noir), or substitute chicken stock

zest and juice of 1 orange

1 ounce (2 tablespoons) inexpensive balsamic vinegar

1 ½ teaspoons grated fresh ginger (or ½ teaspoon ground)

1 teaspoon Sriracha (optional)

¼ teaspoon ground nutmeg

salt and pepper to taste

Melt butter in large saucepan over medium heat; add shallot and cook, stirring, until softened, about 3 to 5 minutes. Add remaining ingredients and bring to a simmer; cook gently about 5 to 10 minutes, or until sauce is reduced slightly and begins to thicken. If meatballs are still baking, remove sauce from heat and cover.

Bring sauce back to simmer over medium heat; gently stir in cooked meatballs to coat with reduction. Reduce heat to medium low and allow to simmer for an additional 5 minutes, stirring occasionally.

Serve hot with pickled cucumbers (page 161) and additional lingonberries.

**MAKES ABOUT 60 TINY MEATBALLS**

# Swedish-Style **Vegan Balls**

Of all the meat-free Swedish balls we enjoyed during my daughter's vegetarian years, this was the best. I like to chop larger ingredients so that the mixture needs only a few pulses in a food processor to make a chunky paste.

2 tablespoons vegetable oil, plus more for frying

1 cup minced onion

1 ½ cups finely chopped shiitake mushrooms

2 cups packed baby spinach

1 tablespoon minced fresh dill

zest and juice of 1 orange, reserve 2 tablespoons of juice for use if mixture is too dry

½ cup whole or halved walnuts, roasted in 350-degree oven about 10 minutes and cooled, then chopped

1 cup panko bread crumbs

¼ cup ground flaxseed (flaxseed meal)

1 cup cooked lentils

2 tablespoons nutritional yeast

1 tablespoon whole-grain mustard

1 teaspoon sea salt

1 teaspoon ground ginger

½ teaspoon pepper

½ teaspoon ground allspice

¼ teaspoon ground nutmeg

In large skillet, warm vegetable oil over medium-high heat and cook onion, stirring often, until it just starts to soften, about 3 minutes. Add mushrooms and continue cooking, stirring often, for an additional 5 minutes. Add spinach and dill and cook until spinach is quite wilted, about 3 to 5 minutes. Add a few tablespoons of the orange juice if mixture gets dry. Season to taste with salt and pepper.

Place all ingredients in food processor and pulse until crumbly paste forms. Add as much orange juice as needed so that the mixture is not too dry. Cool in the refrigerator for 15 to 30 minutes or more.

Using your hands, form balls to desired size and place in a large skillet with a few tablespoons of vegetable oil (enough so balls do not stick). Fry over medium heat, 3 to 4 minutes on each side (alternatively, broil or grill until lightly browned and crisp). Serve with lingonberries and quick-pickled cucumbers (page 161).

**MAKES 4 GENEROUS SERVINGS**
**(38–42 BALLS)**

# Ingebretsen's

In the Twin Cities, there is a common destination for all Minnesotans with a Nordic background: the Norwegian-owned Ingebretsen's. Especially popular during the holidays, Ingebretsen's Nordic Marketplace and Meat Market is standing-room-only throughout December, as we take a number and wait in line to purchase meatball mix, lutefisk, potato sausage, and lingonberries. The beauty of the annual trek is that the crowd is friendly and patient. There is no room for holiday irritability at Ingebretsen's. Instead, we exchange recipes and wish one another Merry Christmas. Ingebretsen's is part of our holiday ritual.

In 1921 Charles Ingebretsen opened Model Meat, which eventually morphed into Ingebretsen's. I spoke with third-generation proprietor Julie Ingebretsen about her family's legacy, asking if she grew up understanding the significance of the store that her grandfather and father built. Julie told me that she understood the importance only recently, and that it has been a gradual process. "It is also concurrent with the development of that importance," she said, explaining that her father, Charles "Bud" Ingebretsen, invited Warren Dahl to become a partner in Ingebretsen's during the 1960s, and that Warren was the one who contributed the famous Swedish meatball mix and sausage recipes to the meat market. It was then that the store started to become identifiably Scandinavian.

Bud and Warren bought the building that houses the store and expanded the small grocery to include a gift shop. "We always had some Norwegian imports, but we weren't a destination for Scandinavian food until Warren."

Julie started working at Ingebretsen's in 1974. At the time, Julie admits, "I had no clue, no interest in business. I guess I forgot to leave." Back then, there were dozens of Scandinavian gift shops around the Twin Cities. Most of those stores eventually disappeared. Changing tastes and an embrace of Scandinavian identity meant a shift in the industry:

from knickknacks and folkcrafts to a modern aesthetic. "People have better taste," Julie joked.

She described the cultural phenomenon so many Scandinavian Americans experience of being stuck in the past, especially with expectations. "We have to keep a balance between the traditional and modern . . . not lose history and what people expect us to have. But cultures evolve. Art evolves; it is a living thing. So is food."

Ten years ago, Ingebretsen's launched an expansion and opened a second gift shop in Stockholm, Wisconsin. Founded by Swedish immigrants, Stockholm is a picturesque village along the banks of the Mississippi River. "It was a big step to venture out of our four walls," Julie said. Ingebretsen's av Stockholm is open weekends and during the summer tourist season.

"My grandfather was born in Sweden, which is sort of a family secret." Julie explained that her grandfather first immigrated to Norway before coming to America. All these years the community has thought of Ingebretsen's as wholly Norwegian. In fact, both of Julie's grandfathers had Swedish ancestry. I asked Julie if she minded my letting the secret out. She laughed and disclosed another family fact: "I grew up Irish. Everything I've learned about Scandinavian culture has come from working at Ingebretsen's, but I like being Irish, too!" Julie's maternal grandmother was an Irish Catholic, and her grandfather converted when they married, as did Julie's dad when he married her mom. "My father used to say that in the fifties and sixties, if customers had known he was Catholic, they might have stopped coming."

Today, both families continue to own the store. Julie manages the gift shop, while Warren's son Steve runs the meat market. Julie's brother, daughter, and nephew also contribute to the store's vitality.

Regarding Ingebretsen's mission, Julie told me that the mission isn't written down but its importance is so great that it is a constant topic of discussion among her family and staff. "Preserving heritage; teaching people where they come from and why that's important. Much of what we do is education based." Julie described her family's commitment to social outreach, especially within the community on East Lake Street. Ingebretsen's is located on a Minneapolis thoroughfare that was historically home to Scandinavian immigrants and now boasts a large Mexican population.

The 1980s brought a transitional period along East Lake Street and in the Powderhorn neighborhood where Ingebretsen's resides. Businesses closed and the neighborhood's reputation took a hit. "When I first got involved with the neighborhood, Lake Street was a boundary." Yet, customers began commenting that they appreciated Ingebretsen's steadfastness, sharing sentiments like, "You are still here! You are here in the world, and this place, in this city, on this street."

In recent years, the East Lake Street community has flourished, with new stores, restaurants, bakeries, and businesses replacing empty buildings with growth and promise. Lake Street has always been a place where immigrants settled, found employment opportunities, established themselves, and contributed not only to the neighborhood but to outer communities as well. Julie explained, "Our responsibility is to do as much as we can to preserve and help."

Rice was not widely available to impoverished Swedes until the late nineteenth century. Barley porridge was more typical fare on Christmas Eve and for other important celebrations.

Traditionally the pudding is a prophetic device: a variety of items are baked into the dish. Bite into an almond and you are to be married, but bite into a bitter almond and you'll become a spinster. Bite into a brown bean and marry a widower or widow. Discover a silver coin and expect wealth.

A bowl of rice pudding is set out on Christmas Eve for the *tomte*, the Santa-like troll that brings gifts that night, as thanks for his protection of the house and family. An empty bowl on Christmas morning predicts peace and prosperity for the coming year.

There are fewer *tomtar* in America, where Santa reigns supreme, and most families leave Santa gifts of cookies rather than rice pudding. As I approached people about contributing recipes to this collection, eight times out of ten I'd be handed a recipe for rice pudding. I began to understand that rice pudding is as important to Swedish celebrations in the heartland as is the meatball.

There are two approaches to Swedish rice pudding. First is the stovetop method (which is occasionally finished in the oven). The resulting pudding is similar to a risotto. Second is the baking method, which commonly includes eggs and is occasionally topped with meringue. Baked pudding is very custard-like, reminiscent of a tapioca in texture. Opinions vary on whether to eat the pudding warm or cold, but all agree that leftover rice pudding makes a sturdy breakfast the morning after a Christmas feast.

# Baked **Rice Pudding**

Faye Olson, Brooklyn Park, Minnesota

"My mother's."

1 cup uncooked rice (do not rinse)

2 cups water

8 cups milk

5 eggs

¾ cup sugar

1 teaspoon salt

½ teaspoon freshly grated nutmeg, plus more for sprinkling

¼–½ cup rum (optional)

In large saucepan, boil rice uncovered in water until absorbed, about 10 minutes. Add milk and continue cooking, uncovered, over low heat until rice breaks down and mixture starts to thicken, about 30 to 45 minutes, stirring occasionally. Remove from heat.

Preheat oven to 300 degrees and grease a large (3-quart) casserole dish (or 9x13–inch cake pan). In mixing bowl, beat eggs with remaining ingredients. Slowly stir in to cooked rice. Pour into prepared casserole and sprinkle top with additional nutmeg if desired. Bake for 40 to 45 minutes or until set. Serve warm or cold.

**SERVES 12**

# Swedish Rice

Gustavus Adolphus College, St. Peter, Minnesota

"This recipe is served annually at the Scandinavian Breakfast, Christmas holiday buffets, and the Festival of St. Lucia luncheon at Gustavus."

4 cups 2 percent milk, divided

pinch salt

¾ cup sugar

2 tablespoons vanilla extract

2 tablespoons cornstarch

⅔ cup egg yolks (about 8 yolks)

2 ¼ cups cooked white rice

In a large saucepan, heat 3 cups milk to 180 degrees. Stir in salt, sugar, and vanilla. Bring back to 180 degrees. Combine cornstarch with remaining 1 cup of milk and add to hot milk, then bring back to 180 degrees.

In medium bowl, whisk egg yolks to combine. Slowly whisk in 1 cup of the hot milk mixture. Add yolk mixture to hot milk mixture and return to 175 degrees. Add cooked rice and stir to combine. Chill in refrigerator overnight. If necessary, add some half-and-half or milk to thin before serving in individual sauce dishes or in large bowl on buffet.

SERVES 12

# Carole
## ARWIDSON

## GUSTAVUS ADOLPHUS CLASS OF 1984

As Swedish immigrants to this country, my family has always been bilingual and bicultural. For us, that has meant that our holiday celebrations are very Swedish in their traditions and rituals. As a little girl, I quickly realized that there are differences, such as the fact that Swedish children wait up and greet the *tomte* (the Swedish version of Santa Claus) as he comes into the home to deliver *julklappar* (Christmas gifts). (This caused great confusion for me as a child when I heard my friends say they had never met Santa. I don't think they ever believed my story.) There was much anticipation on every *julafton* (Christmas Eve) as we finished eating a traditional lutfisk dinner and eagerly waited for the doorbell to ring, announcing the *tomte's* arrival (as it turns out, the *tomte* was my older sister, cleverly disguised).

As wonderful as those moments, and now memories, were, I do believe that my mother, Sigbritt, had the more magical experience on *julafton*. My mother was born in Gränsjön, a small farming village in the forest in the province of Värmland, the youngest of eight children. The farm was nestled in a clearing in the forest and reached by a long, winding gravel driveway from the main road. The house sat closest to the road (though you couldn't see it from the road), with a big red barn tucked back up against the forest's mighty trees. On *julafton*, with deep snow surrounding the house, which was softly lit inside though pitch dark outside save for any starlight, my aunt Ingegerd, one of my mom's older sisters, "played the *tomten*." Ingegerd would sneak out after dinner to don gray woolen pants and a coat, a beard, and a red woolen hat. She made her way quietly into the dark forest, emerging magically from the tall trees bearing a candlelit lantern in one hand to guide her way, the other holding the sack of gifts over her shoulder. That must have been an incredible sight to see—especially for a child—and no doubt brought a bit of magic to the Christmas festivities.

# Sigbritt's *Risgrynspudding* (Swedish Rice Pudding)

From Carole Arwidson and her mother, Sigbritt Arwidson, Minneapolis, Minnesota

"It is tradition in Sweden to eat rice pudding as part of the Christmas celebration, and it is something my family and I continue to do to this day. While *lutfisk* is the traditional evening meal for our family on *julafton*, rice pudding is a dish we have as part of the *julbord* (Christmas season smorgasbord), which we enjoy earlier in the day. This recipe for Sigbritt's *Risgrynspudding* (Sigbritt's Rice Pudding) was handed down to my mother from her mother—my *mormor* (grandmother)—and then on to me."

1½ cups long-cooking rice

dash salt

4–6 cups milk

1 tablespoon margarine

2 eggs

1 cup sugar

1 ½ cups *vaniljsocker* (Swedish vanilla sugar; see tip page 12)

raisins (optional)

lingonberries and heavy cream for serving

Place rice in double boiler or heavy-bottomed pot on the stovetop. Add salt and pour in enough milk to cover the rice. Stir to mix in the salt. Place margarine on top of the milk mixture. Bring to a boil and then cook on low heat, continuously stirring and adding milk as needed. It will take about 1½ to 2 hours to cook the rice; keep a close eye on the double boiler, as the rice will quickly burn and stick to the bottom if there is not enough milk. When rice is soft, pour mixture into a large bowl and let cool (see tip).

Preheat oven to 350 degrees and grease a large (3-quart) glass baking dish. In a large mixing bowl, whisk together the eggs and sugar. Add the *vaniljsocker* and stir. Combine this mixture with the rice and mix together with a wooden spoon. (If the mixture is too thick and dense, add another egg. If it is still too thick, add some milk.) Add raisins, as many as desired. The mixture should be sweet: taste to determine if more sugar is needed. Pour the mixture into the prepared baking dish. Bake for 1 hour, until the top is lightly browned. Let the pudding sit for about 5 minutes before serving topped with lingonberries and heavy cream.

SERVES 12

 **TIP:** The rice can be prepared the day before. Bring to room temperature before preparing the mixture for baking.

# Rice Pudding

Kristine Bolander, the Bolander Family, in memory of Dorothy, David, Alice, and Ivar, with special thanks to Mae Bolander, Minneapolis, Minnesota

1 cup long grain rice

about 4 cups milk

2–3 cinnamon sticks

2 eggs, separated

pinch salt

¼–½ cup sugar

6–8 cardamom seeds, crushed

Place rice, milk, and cinnamon sticks in large pot and cook over low to medium heat, stirring constantly, until rice has absorbed a quantity of milk and is done to taste, about 40 minutes.

Preheat oven to 325 degrees and grease a 2-quart casserole dish. Beat egg yolks. In a separate bowl, beat egg whites to soft peaks. Add a cup of hot rice to a large mixing bowl. Stir in beaten egg yolks, salt, sugar to taste, and cardamom. Add back to rice mixture. Gently fold in beaten egg whites. Pour into prepared casserole and bake, uncovered, for 30 minutes.

**SERVES 8**

# Swedish **Rice Pudding**

Lynn Moore, Bemidji, Minnesota

---

"Grandma Lero prepared Swedish Rice Pudding every Christmas Eve. She slipped an almond into the pudding, and the person who found the almond had good luck for the year.

"Grandma Lero was my husband's grandmother, and she immigrated at sixteen. This is her recipe and the one she passed on to me. I always loved the idea of finding the almond. When he was a small child, this simple rice pudding was a favorite of my son. We did carry on the Christmas Eve tradition.

"Rice pudding is one of those controversial *julbord* dishes that divides families. Baked versus boiled, eggs versus eggless, cream versus milk, almond versus coin: everyone has an opinion about what constitutes the perfect rice pudding or *risgrynsgröt*. This recipe updates old traditions, and perhaps will give your diners something new to debate at the Christmas table."

1 cup rice

4 ¾ cups milk

6 eggs

¾ cup sugar

1 cup raisins (optional)

cinnamon sugar for serving

Preheat oven to 350 degrees and grease a 9x13–inch pan. In saucepan, cook rice in ¾ cup water and ¾ cup milk for 15 minutes over medium-high heat, adding additional water ½ cup at a time if rice becomes dry.

In large mixing bowl, beat eggs. Stir in remaining 4 cups milk, sugar, and raisins (if using), then add cooked rice and continue beating until well combined. Pour into prepared pan and bake for 50 to 60 minutes, until inserted knife comes out clean. Sprinkle with cinnamon sugar.

SERVES 8

# Coconut Barley Pudding
## (*Pärlgryn Gröt*)

¾ cup barley

2 (14-ounce) cans coconut milk

1 vanilla bean, halved and seeded

1 cinnamon stick

2 tablespoons sugar

zest and juice of 1 small lime

handful dried cranberries or raisins

half-and-half or pineapple juice

grated coconut, toasted, for serving

freshly grated nutmeg for serving

Rinse raw barley in cold water. Place in large saucepan and cover with 6 cups water. Bring to boil and simmer, covered, 15 minutes. Drain barley and return it to the saucepan.

Stir in coconut milk, vanilla seeds and bean, cinnamon stick, sugar, lime juice, and cranberries or raisins. Bring to simmer; cook, covered, on low until barley is tender and milk has thickened, about 30 to 40 minutes, stirring occasionally. Remove cover during final 10 minutes of cook time and add half-and-half or pineapple juice if pudding becomes dry. Remove vanilla bean and cinnamon stick. Garnish with lime zest, toasted grated coconut, and nutmeg.

**SERVES 6–8**

# Risgrynsgröt

Eva Sabet, Anoka, Minnesota

⅔ cup Swedish porridge rice (or substitute sushi or Arborio rice)

1 ¼ cups water

1 teaspoon sea salt

2 ½ cups milk

¾ cup organic heavy cream (see tip)

2 tablespoons butter

1 tablespoon sugar

1 long or 2 short cinnamon sticks

Use a large pot with a thick bottom or enameled cast iron. Place rice in colander and rinse with cold water until the water runs clear. Place rice in pot and add water and salt and bring to a boil; cover and cook over medium heat for exactly 10 minutes.

Add milk, cream, butter, sugar, and cinnamon stick(s) and give rice a good stir. Make sure rice is not sticking to bottom of the pot. Bring to a quick boil and immediately set heat to lowest possible setting; simmer rice, covered, for 45 to 60 minutes. Stir rice every 10 to 20 minutes to make sure it is not sticking and that the heat is not so high that the rice is boiling.

Rice is cooked when it is nicely swollen and tender to your teeth. Remove from heat and allow to cool and thicken. Serve warm or cold with jam, cinnamon sugar, or *saftsas* (fruit sauce made with berry juice and thickened with starch).

**SERVES 6**

 **TIP:** Do not use cream with additives such as xanthan or guar gum, as these can cause separation in porridge.

*five*

JULBORD

# Smörgåsbord is one

of very few Swedish words so valuable to our American culture that it has become part of our language. The buffet of many tables is a special occasion, whether served at home or, more commonly, in restaurants. *Smörgåsbord* translates as sandwich table (or bread and butter table), a modest title for an amazing banquet of fancy dishes.

*Smörgåsbord* is the grandchild of *brännvinsbord* (the burning wine table or spirits table). *Brännvinsbord* was an appetizer course consisting of bread and butter served with beer in wealthy homes before a meal. As the caraway spirit aquavit became important to Swedish cuisine in the 1700s, it was added to the *brännvinsbord*, along with bread, butter, salted and cured fish, meat, and cheese. Known as SOS (*smör, ost och sill*—butter, cheese, and herring), the expanded *brännvinsbord* is now seen at the first table, also called the herring or fish course, of modern *smörgåsbord*.

As SOS became popular, so too did the practice of presenting an entire meal on the table rather than plated service, not unlike what we refer to as service family-style. Modern *smörgåsbord* spread from these customs during the 1880s, when travel by train increased, as did the need for lodging and public dining. At the same time, new methods in food preservation allowed an abundant feast where out-of-season delicacies appeared alongside seasonal dishes. The popularity of *smörgåsbord* continued until World War II, when food shortages caused the government to prohibit it.

Several decades passed before the *smörgåsbord* became common. Now, food is placed on a separate table or tables, and diners leave their seated places to collect foods from one buffet, then return to their dining tables to eat, progressing from each course to the next and using a clean plate each time. Each course is washed down with aquavit, beer, coffee, and, at *jul*, *punsch*.

*Julbord* is the holiday version of *smörgåsbord*. Along with the salmon and herring, salads, roasts and meatballs, and desserts are special Christmas foods such as ham, lingonberries, and Jansson's Temptation. Elaborate settings will have many tables, but smaller venues combine themes (herring and seafood may share space, as can the cold table with cheese).

### COURSE ONE
## *herring table*

There is never too much herring, whether pickled, smoked, dilled, or creamed. This table also includes accompaniments such as hot boiled potatoes, boiled eggs, sharp tangy cheeses, and rye bread and crackers.

### COURSE TWO
## *seafood*

This table typically celebrates gravlax with an assortment of mustard sauces, hot smoked or poached salmon, oysters, and garnishes of roe, sour cream or crème fraîche, onion, and shrimp.

### COURSE THREE
## *cold table*

Vegetable and fruit salads, pâté, and cold cuts.

### COURSE FOUR
## *hot table*

Swedish meatballs with lingonberries, sausages, *sylta*, warm ham, Jansson's, brown beans, cabbage.

### COURSE FIVE
## *cheese*

A variety of cheeses.

### COURSE SIX
## *dessert*

Rice pudding, fruit soup, *ostkaka*, caramel pudding.

In America, we haven't quite figured it out. I've dined with friends and family who rush to the hot meat table and then load salads and fish next to their meatballs, piling their plates with as much food as they think they can manage. I wince with embarrassment at their bad form. Perhaps I learned proper *smörgåsbord* etiquette when my family ate at the Jolly Troll, or perhaps I've heard enough from my Swedish friends that I wouldn't dare break the rules when it comes to my beloved *smörgåsbord*. (At any rate, my parents were big on manners: family lore tells of a time one sister accidentally spilled her drink at a drive-in burger place and we never returned because my dad was so mortified.)

We didn't go out to eat much when I was a kid, except when we visited Grandpa Johnson in Minneapolis. Grandpa loved dining out, and I've never been sure which appealed to him most: eating the food or flirting with the pretty waitresses.

When my older sisters and I swap stories about events from our youth, none of us agree on any of the details. One thing we do agree on is that when we dined out it was usually at the Jolly Troll. At least one time, anyway.

Susan recalls, "I remember being at the Jolly Troll at least four times for sure. I remember Grandpa and Grandma [Johnson] being along twice."

But our mom remembers differently. "When we went to the Jolly Troll, it was just our family. I don't remember going more than once, and I don't think Grandpa was with us. At that time, he was living in Cambridge," she said.

Yet, if we went to the Jolly Troll only once, how can our memories of those trolls remain so vivid? Susan told me, "I was totally fascinated with the trolls. I felt like having to bother with eating was an unnecessary distraction. The Jell-O was served in a square piece! I had never seen anything like that before in my whole life! It was mind-boggling to me. But the trolls, those magical moving little puppets: I could've lived there and never eaten a thing. It was all about the trolls. Each time we went, I would discover something new that the trolls were doing. It was just a beautiful, magical place. When I close my eyes, I can tell you where the trolls were and what they were doing."

I was not even in school yet when we dined at the Jolly Troll, but the impression the mechanical little men left on me is as real as if I were watching them attending to their tasks even now. There was a kitchen troll standing on a step stool to stir a pot of bubbling soup. Another little man sliced rye bread. In the yard two trolls sawed lumber. The trolls moved with the quirky, jerky motions of puppets, but I could see they were alive even as I pressed my chin up against the partition that separated us.

I've always had an appetite, and the dining room smells eventually lured me away from the trolls. My childhood eyes remember endless buffet tables that spilled over with mountains of meatballs, ham, potatoes, and desserts (including those squares of Jell-O and custard). There are some events even more magical than mechanical trolls.

It never occurred to me that those trolls were another little girl's siblings.

I met Carole Jean Anderson for lunch at Fika, the café at the American Swedish Institute in Minneapolis. I'd read an article about her in our local daily newspaper. The Jolly Troll heiress: what a glorious title. As we began our conversation, Carole Jean told me about coming to the American Swedish Institute as a child. "We would come to Santa Lucia at ASI early in the morning. I remember always wishing I could wear the crown."

While Carole Jean looks back fondly at her years working at her parents' buffet restaurant, she wasn't as enraptured with the trolls as tiny diners were. When Carole Jean was a teen, she shared her bedroom space with convalescing and

retired trolls, and yes, it was a little creepy, especially when she had to explain the trolls to friends.

Carole Jean's dad, Ray A. Anderson, got the idea to open a *smörgåsbord* restaurant after he and Carole Jean's mom, Alice, visited Scandinavia in the 1960s. From the buffet-style service and Scandinavian-inspired foods to the trolls and server uniforms (based on the regional costumes of the Nordic countries), Ray and Alice brought more than just a taste of Sweden back to Minnesota. In the most Swedish of all states, Jolly Troll gained an easy popularity. Neighboring Wisconsin, Iowa, and even Indiana joined the buffet buzz as Ray sold shares of the business. Jolly Troll moved as far west as Seattle, where Carole Jean's brother took the reins for a short time until the 1980s, when all-you-can-eat establishments began to lose popularity.

Chef Rodney Herzog ran the kitchen at the Golden Valley location and used his personal recipes for most of the food he served, including his famous Swedish meatballs, rice pudding, and coleslaw. Carole Jean recalls lines out the door, especially during the holidays, when lutfisk was added to the substantial Jolly Troll menu.

At home, the Christmas menu was no less extensive. Carole Jean rattled off a long list of treats that always appeared on the Anderson *julbord*: "In early December Mom and Grandma began baking . . . so many cookies! Raspberry ribbons, *pepparkakor*, *skorpa*." For Christmas Eve, "There was pickled pigs feet, *sylta*, potato sausage, *knäckbröd*, limpa, herring, beets, potatoes with butter, ham, meatballs with cream, and lutfisk." There were also two rice puddings: one prepared on the stovetop that included cinnamon sticks and an almond, and one baked in the oven, then served with lingonberries. Carole Jean recalled that on Christmas morning the family ate "Swedish coffee bread that was braided and decorated with pearl sugar. I could eat eight *bullar*!"

Ray was a lover of all things Christmas. "He was driven to do everything for Christmas. Then we'd have a whole Thanksgiving-like meal with turkey on Christmas Day. We'd drive around and look at Christmas windows and the Dayton's display. My grandmother would always dress up. Having family around was so special. When I was a kid, my dad would read "The Christmas Story," and then we opened presents. After that we'd have our rice pudding and cookies, and then we'd go to church. It was always a rush."

Carole Jean confided that she still owns several trolls. She invited me to meet them on a cold January morning. We chatted over hot coffee and treats from

my neighborhood Scandinavian bakery, and when it was finally time, Carole Jean led me to a storage room, unlocked the door, and turned on the light.

A dozen trolls stood tending their tasks, as they had been doing for fifty years: lost in their responsibilities, lost in time. The guys (and one gal holding a chicken) were a little worse for wear. I walked among the rows of trolls, touching one or two sweet faces gently, smoothing a beard and tucking a sleeve. The men are slightly torn, a little dusty, but still smiling and oh so magical. There were trolls wearing chef's jackets slicing rye bread, and two of them stirred something brown in a pot. A headless troll climbed a ladder to nowhere, and a rather happy-looking fellow held his flowering pot, ready to garden.

It is not exaggeration (much) to say that I felt as if my entire life had led to this moment. Here stood a dozen little sprites, evidence that my childhood memories did not come from an overactive imagination. It was a "Yes, Virginia" sort of epiphany.

> Yes, Patrice, there are Jolly Trolls. They exist as certainly as love of buffets and family celebrations. Alas! How dreary would be the world if there were no Jolly Trolls. No Jolly Trolls! Thank God! They live, and live forever (or until the last of our generation is gone and the mechanical trolls are, sadly, forgotten). A dozen years from now, Patrice, nay, ten times a dozen years from now, they will continue to make glad the memories of childhood.

While Ray, Alice, Carole Jean's brother, and even Chef Rodney have passed on, the trolls remain. They live in Carole Jean's storage, still tending to their tasks of slicing rye bread and stirring something tasty in a pot, waiting to charm children.

## Not-So-Devilish **Eggs with Gravlax**

12 eggs, hardcooked and peeled

½ cup crème fraîche (recipe follows)

1 ½ tablespoons capers, rinsed and chopped roughly

several tablespoons minced fresh dill, plus additional sprigs for serving

several tablespoons minced fresh chives, plus additional sprigs for serving

2 teaspoons lemon juice

2 teaspoons horseradish

pepper

¼–½ cup gravlax, diced or cubed

caviar or roe

flaked salt to finish, if desired

Slice eggs in half lengthwise. Remove yolks and place in medium mixing bowl. Place whites on a serving dish.

Use a fork to mash the yolks into a fine crumble. Add crème fraîche, capers, minced herbs, lemon juice, horseradish, and pepper to taste; mix well. Gently fold in gravlax. Spoon a heaping teaspoon of the gravlax mixture into each egg white. Garnish with caviar, herb sprigs, and flaked salt.

**MAKES 24**

## Crème Fraîche

1 cup heavy cream

2 tablespoons buttermilk

2 tablespoons full-fat Greek-style yogurt

Stir together ingredients in glass dish and cover with paper towel attached with rubber band; set out at room temperature for 18 to 24 hours. Stir or shake, then chill.

**MAKES 1 ¼ CUPS**

Not-So-Devilish Eggs with Gravlax

## Pickled **Red Beets**

1 large red beet, peeled and cut into half-inch cubes or quarter-inch slices

¾ cup water

¾ cup sugar

¾ cup white vinegar

½ star anise

10 red peppercorns

5 allspice berries

1 teaspoon salt

Add all ingredients to small pot and simmer until beets are tender, about 15 to 20 minutes depending on size of beet chunks. Chill before serving. Use within a week.

**Other optional seasonings:** cinnamon, nutmeg, cardamom, brown sugar

SERVES 4–6

## Pickled **Golden Beets**

1 large golden beet, peeled and cut into half-inch cubes or quarter-inch slices

¾ cup sugar

¾ cup water

¾ cup white vinegar

zest and juice of 1 orange

1 teaspoon caraway seeds

1 teaspoon fennel seeds

1 teaspoon salt

Add all ingredients to small pot and simmer until beets are tender, about 15 to 20 minutes depending on size of beet chunks. Chill before serving. Use within a week.

**Other optional seasonings:** ginger, tarragon, raw fennel bulb sliced very thin

SERVES 4–6

# *Pressgurka* (Quick-Pickled Cucumbers)

1 cup white vinegar

1 cup sugar

1 teaspoon caraway seeds

1 teaspoon salt

1 bay leaf

1 ½ cups ice

2 English cucumbers, sliced thin

½ cup thinly sliced red onion (optional)

2 tablespoons fresh and 1 teaspoon dried dill (see note)

Combine the vinegar, sugar, caraway, salt, and bay leaf in a medium saucepan and boil over medium-high heat until the sugar dissolves, about 5 minutes. Add the ice and cool pickling liquid until ice is completely melted.

Place cucumbers, onion (if using), and dill in clean canning jars or glass bowl. Pour brine over the solids and chill for 2 hours or up to a week before serving.

**MAKES 3–4 CUPS**

 **NOTE:** A smart Swedish caterer once told me that she combines fresh and dried dill in all of her dishes. The two provide very different and unique flavors that together form a perfect combination.

# *Sill* **Salad** (Herring Salad)

Adapted from recipe by Bruce Karstadt's mother, Patty Karstadt, Lindsborg, Kansas

Garnish with sliced hardcooked eggs and parsley. Serve with additional whipped cream colored with beet juice if desired.

1 pint pickled herring, onions and seasonings removed, fish rinsed well

1 cup chopped pickled beets

1 ½ cups chopped boiled potatoes

1 ½ cups chopped apples

¼ cup chopped onion

⅓ cup chopped sweet pickles

¼ cup white vinegar

2 tablespoons sugar

2 tablespoons water

1 ½ teaspoons salt

½ teaspoon pepper

½ cup whipping cream, whipped (optional)

In mixing bowl, combine herring, beets, potatoes, apples, onion, and pickles. In separate bowl, whisk together vinegar, sugar, water, salt, and pepper. If using whipped cream, fold into the whisked dressing. Add dressing to solids mixture and gently fold together.

SERVES 6–8

# Smoked Fish Salad with Mustard Sauce

Kerstin Trowbridge, Swedish American Heritage Society
of West Michigan, Grand Rapids, Michigan

3 tablespoons mustard (preferably
Swedish Slotts Senap or IKEA's mild)

3 tablespoons white wine vinegar

3 tablespoons sugar

10 tablespoons canola oil

1 large crisp apple, chopped

1 medium onion, chopped (Vidalia is nice)

4 ½ ounces smoked fish (salmon or chub),
in a chunk (Morey's works well), flaked

fresh chives or dill for serving

Stir together mustard, vinegar, and sugar.
Add oil a tablespoon at a time. Mix well. Place
chopped apple, then onion, and last flaked
smoked fish in a serving dish. Pour mustard
sauce over (see tip). Refrigerate salad and serve
as part of a *smörgåsbord* or as an appetizer.
Garnish with fresh chives or dill.

SERVES 4

  **TIP:** Use leftover sauce as salad dressing, for another
batch of the smoked fish salad, on green beans or
gravlax. Chill and keep up to a week in the refrigerator.

Smoked Fish Salad with Mustard Sauce (page 163)

*Julskinka* (page 178) with Lingonberry Mostarda (page 165)

# Lingonberry Mostarda

1 cup granulated sugar

½ cup packed brown sugar

½ cup champagne vinegar

½ cup water

¼ cup yellow mustard seeds

3 tablespoons maple syrup or honey

2 cups fresh or frozen lingonberries

3 tablespoons prepared Dijon mustard

zest of 1 orange

salt and pepper to taste

In large saucepan, combine sugars, vinegar, water, mustard seeds, and syrup. Bring to a boil, reduce heat, and simmer, uncovered, for 15 minutes, stirring occasionally. Add 1 cup lingonberries and continue simmering, stirring frequently, for additional 15 minutes. Add remaining berries and simmer another 10 minutes. Remove from heat and stir in Dijon mustard, zest, salt, and pepper. Chill and serve.

**MAKES ABOUT 4 CUPS**

# Hot Mustard Sauce
## for Smoked Oysters or other...

Gustavus Adolphus College, St. Peter, Minnesota

"There is NOTHING bland about this hot mustard sauce. Perfect for dipping smoked oysters or a drizzle on a smoked salmon canapé. This sauce accompanies much on the holiday *smörgäsbords* at Gustavus!"

¼ cup dry mustard

¼ cup white vinegar

¼ cup sugar

¼ teaspoon salt

1 egg

Mix dry mustard and vinegar; cover and chill overnight. Place mustard-vinegar mixture in saucepan and mix in sugar, salt, and egg. Slowly bring to a simmer and heat until sauce is thickened and coats a spoon. Serve warm or cold . . . we like warm!

**SERVES 12**

If you spot me at your local *julbord*, you'd best push me out of the way if you intend to eat at the fish table. I am greedy and gather up all the gravlax and herring I can fit on my plate, leaving the Jansson's for the folks who like to fill up on starches. That first buffet of cold fish dishes and cheese and eggs is the big ticket in my foodie opinion, and I can hardly wait to enjoy every morsel.

Gravlax was originally called gravad lax, or buried salmon, as the fish was buried while it cured. The cure time depends on the thickness of your salmon.

For variety, use a fish other than salmon. As long as the fish you cure is fatty, your results will be amazing. I like to cube gravlax. While thin slices of the salmon shows off its silky texture, cubing it brings a whole new bite to the experience, and, if you don't own a decent fillet knife, it is easier to cut cubes. Whatever you decide, do not waste the cured skin! Slice it into strips and pan-fry it for a fun salmon chip to add as a garnish or to eat by yourself over the pan when no one is looking.

When preparing cured salmon at home, I typically emphasize the flavors of the season. At *jul*, tangerines are abundant, so I add them to the sugar, salt, pepper, and dill cure. Add that same citrus flavor to mustard sauce, and serve the salmon with little salads of tangerine sections and fennel. ✍

# Tangerine Gravlax

2 cups sugar

1 cup kosher salt

2 tablespoons freshly ground pepper

several sprigs dill

1 ½ pounds sushi-quality salmon fillet, skin on

1–2 tangerines, sliced

Combine dry ingredients and rub into salmon on both sides. Lay salmon in glass dish and completely encase in the salt and dill mixture. Place tangerine slices over mixture. Wrap in plastic and allow to rest at room temperature 4 to 6 hours. Place weight over salmon to push the moisture out of the fish and yield a silky texture. Refrigerate salmon an additional 36 hours, flipping fish every 12 hours. The cure will liquefy during curing process. Rinse salmon, pat dry with paper towels, and slice paper thin. Use within a few days.

SERVES 6–8

# Aquavit-Cured Gravlax

8 ounces salmon

½ cup sugar

¼ cup kosher salt

2 teaspoons dried dill

zest of 1 orange

2 tablespoons Gamle Ode dill aquavit or other clean-flavored spirit such as vodka or tequila

Cover the salmon in the sugar, salt, dill, and zest. Spritz with aquavit. Pack in plastic and weigh down with heavy dish or pan. Refrigerate 48 hours, turning every 12. Rinse or wipe cure from salmon. Slice thin or cube for serving and use within a few days.

SERVES 2–4 AS AN APPETIZER

# Apple *Kaka*

Jane Sallstrom Grams, from her grandmother Sigrid Monson, Winthrop, Minnesota

"We serve this at every holiday as it is a favorite of our entire family."

3 cups crushed rusk (see page 82)

¾ cup (1 ½ sticks) butter, melted

4 cups applesauce

2 teaspoons cinnamon

½ cup sugar

Preheat oven to 350 degrees and grease a 2-quart casserole dish. Combine rusk with butter. In a separate bowl, stir together applesauce, cinnamon, and sugar. Layer half the crumbs, all of the applesauce, and the other half of the crumbs in prepared casserole. Bake, uncovered, for 30 to 45 minutes.

SERVES 6–8

# Gloria & Mariann's *story*

I met MariAnn Tiblin when we were volunteers together at a potato sausage–making class at the American Swedish Institute in Minneapolis. Our duties were to supervise each station and ensure the students were following directions as they mixed spices and raw meat, pushed the mixture into stinky, slippery intestines, and tied off the ends. Spritely MariAnn seemed to know everyone and hustled between tables to inspect sausage and encourage the casing stuffers. I weighed the links and divvied them up into plastic bags for each participant, certain that after witnessing that meat madness I would not soon again enjoy potato sausage.

MariAnn came to Minnesota from Sweden in her youth to run the Swedish Collections at the University of Minnesota. Still a Swedish citizen, she nonetheless remains in Minnesota post-retirement. MariAnn introduced me to her friend Gloria Hawkinson.

Gloria arrived in Minnesota in the 1950s, when her husband became pastor at Grace Lutheran (on the University of Minnesota campus). "I was raised in Rockford, Illinois. I had four sisters and four brothers and a mother and father who were both born in Sweden," Gloria told me. "They came over as children from Västergötland. They met in Rockford." Gloria was born in 1921, the eighth of nine children. "My older brothers and sisters learned Swedish, but by the time I came along my parents mostly just used it when they didn't want us to know what they were talking about."

Gloria's mother baked rice pudding in the oven, and the family often enjoyed it as a dessert, not just at Christmas. At Christmas they also enjoyed caramel pudding.

"*Brylépudding* is what we say in Swedish. That's caramel pudding," MariAnn told us.

Gloria added, "I remember being served a dinner once down in Mexico City. They wanted to have a typical Mexican dessert, and I said, 'It is just like my Swedish mother used to make!'" She added, "'It is very Swedish,' I said."

The cashier at the café where we were chatting was sitting close enough to listen to our conversation, and she interrupted, "No, no, my mother called it Swedish pudding or *weddingris*." *Ris* is Swedish for rice, and I assumed she was referring to rice pudding, but she continued. "With caramel in the bottom: custard."

MariAnn asked the cashier what she called the pudding in Swedish.

"*Brölle*," the cashier answered.

"*Brölle*. Yes, that's brûlée," MariAnn rolled the words with her Swedish accent, and we heard the similarity.

"Wedding pudding!" I was proud to show off my limited but occasionally useful knowledge of Swedish.

"Oh, that's funny!" MariAnn chuckled at the journey of the custard's name. The French word "brûlée" was pronounced *brölle* in Swedish, which became *bröllopudding*. "*Bröllop*" is Swedish for wedding. So the American family called their Swedish brûlée "wedding pudding."

MariAnn interjected and reminded Gloria, "Don't forget the sausage!"

"When it came time for Christmas, this was when I was a young girl, my mother would buy half a pig, and out of that she would make sausage and she would make it with barley. Not with potatoes like they do up in Minnesota but with barley," Gloria recalled.

It wasn't until a few years after my first funky sausage-making session that I found myself in my friend Tiffany's kitchen where she and our sausage-making buddy John set up an enormous meat grinder. Hog casings, raw meat, onions, and allspice were the aroma of the day. Sausage making is not pretty, and it doesn't smell so great. However, the experience becomes fun if you add good friends and a Bloody Mary or two.

We stuffed dozens of casings, enough to share and plenty to freeze for summer grilling. When we cooked up samples from each batch, Gloria's barley sausage was the hit of the party.

---

# Barley **Korv** (Sausage)

As handwritten by Gloria Hawkinson,
formerly of Minneapolis, Minnesota

4 pounds pork
shoulder, ground

3 cups cooked barley — not
ground or pearl

2 medium sweet
white onions, minced

2 teaspoons salt

2 teaspoons pepper

1 teaspoon ground allspice

Mix all ingredients very well.
Use instructions provided by
manufacturer to fill hog casings.
Alternatively, form large patties.

**MAKES 20 LARGE SAUSAGES**

# *Bruna Bönor* (Brown Beans)

Patty Karstadt, Lindsborg, Kansas

I was never so much a fan of brown beans as I was of the elegant vinegar carafe my mom placed on the dinner table next to the bean dish. I loved how the tart vinegar made my mouth pucker, and I especially loved being allowed to pour the vinegar from the carafe, all by myself. Serve Patty's brown beans with vinegar on the side if you like to pucker, too.

My friend farmer Paula Foreman donated her crop of Swedish brown beans to me for this recipe. They were the most tender, flavorful, nutty beans I've ever tasted. If you are lucky enough to know a farmer willing to provide beans to this endeavor, be grateful! If you cannot find brown beans, fava or lima beans will suffice, or use your favorite dried bean.

1 ½ cups brown beans (see head note)

2 teaspoons salt

½ cup molasses

2 tablespoons white vinegar

½ cup packed brown sugar

Rinse beans and soak in 1 ½ quarts water overnight. Place beans and soaking water into large stockpot. Water should cover beans by an inch; add more water if needed. Bring beans to a boil, then immediately lower the heat to a gentle simmer. Cook, uncovered, until the beans are tender, about 2 hours, adding more water as needed to keep the beans covered by an inch of water. Remove any foam from surface as it collects. Do not allow beans to boil. Season to taste with salt, molasses, vinegar, and brown sugar.

**SERVES 4–6**

# Baked **Red Cabbage**

Eva Sabet, Anoka, Minnesota

---

**"Eat as a side dish with ham, meatballs, or *prinskorv* [small Swedish sausages] or by itself if vegetarian. This can be done with regular cabbage as well."**

If using white cabbage, omit bay leaf and use 1–2 teaspoons allspice instead.

½ cup (1 stick) salted butter (preferably European butter)

2 ½ pounds red cabbage, shredded

½ cup Swedish light or dark syrup (you can substitute corn syrup but do not use molasses)

¼ cup apple cider vinegar

1 bay leaf (see head note)

salt and pepper

Preheat oven to 350 degrees. Set a large skillet over maximum heat and add butter. When butter is melted, add half the cabbage. Keep the heat high so cabbage doesn't release too much juice, and stir frequently so it doesn't burn. Cook about 5 minutes. When the first batch of cabbage has wilted in the pan, add in the rest of the cabbage and the syrup, vinegar, and bay leaf. Reduce heat to medium and continue cooking and stirring, about 20 minutes.

When the cabbage is completely wilted, transfer to a large (2 ½–quart) baking dish and bake for 60 to 75 minutes or until cabbage is soft and shiny, stirring every 20 minutes. If cabbage gets too much color or dries out, cover with foil. Cabbage should not be crispy or mushy. If it is too dry, add more butter. Season with salt and pepper to taste.

**SERVES 4**

# Corn Pudding

Carole Jean Anderson, Minneapolis, Minnesota

4 eggs

2 cups milk

1 (14 ¾–ounce) can cream-style corn

2–3 tablespoons flour

1 tablespoon sugar

1 teaspoon salt

½ teaspoon pepper

2–3 tablespoons butter

3 tablespoons dried bread crumbs

Preheat oven to 375 degrees and grease a 1 ½–quart casserole dish. In large mixing bowl, whisk together eggs and milk. Add corn, flour, sugar, salt, and pepper, stirring to combine. Pour mixture into prepared pan. Dot with dabs of butter and sprinkle with bread crumbs. Place casserole in larger pan and fill outer pan with 1 inch of water or halfway up casserole. Bake for 45 to 60 minutes, until knife inserted in the center comes out clean.

SERVES 10

# *Fruktsoppa* (Fruit Soup)

Jane Sallstrom Grams's mother, Margaret Monson, Winthrop, Minnesota

"We serve this every Christmas Eve right after church and before supper. This recipe has been handed down to me from generations. I am 100 percent Swedish. My dad's (Ray Sallstrom's) grandparents came to the state in 1853 and my mother's (Margaret Monson's) grandparents came in 1871."

1 (8-ounce) bag prunes

1 cup raisins

4 ounces (about ⅔ cup) dried apricots

¼ cup tapioca

1 cup sugar

1 cinnamon stick

1 (8-ounce) jar maraschino cherries, drained

Soak the prunes, raisins, and apricots overnight in water.

In large stockpot, stir together fruit, soaking water, tapioca, sugar, and cinnamon stick along with enough water to cover ingredients by 1 inch. Cook over medium-high heat until the fruit is soft and just begins to break apart, about 45 minutes. Add cherries. Serve hot.

SERVES 8–10

# *Janssons Frestelse* (Jansson's Temptation)

Kerstin Trowbridge, Swedish American Heritage Society of
West Michigan, Grand Rapids, Michigan

For a proper Jansson's, Swedish sprats rather than Italian anchovies must be used. Unlike common anchovies with their overpowering salty fish taste, sprats (known as *ansjovis*) are mild and sweet. If you cannot find them in your local fish and specialty stores, order online.

5–6 medium potatoes, peeled and cut into thin batons

1 (4.4-ounce) tin Swedish *ansjovis* (anchovy-style sprats; see head note), undrained

1 medium yellow onion, chopped and cooked in a little butter

1 cup heavy cream or half-and-half

2 tablespoons bread crumbs

Preheat oven to 400 degrees. Layer half of potatoes on bottom of greased 8x8–inch casserole. Arrange sprat fillets evenly on top along with cooked onion. Top with remaining potatoes. Drizzle top with a little of the sprat brine, 1 tablespoon or so. Pour cream over all. Cream should reach the top layer of potatoes but not cover them. Sprinkle top with bread crumbs. Bake for about 50 minutes or until potatoes are soft and top is browned.

**SERVES 4**

# *Julskinka* (Christmas Ham)

Pairs well with Lingonberry Mostarda (page 165).

3–4 pound ham, cooked and cooled

2 tablespoons panko bread crumbs

2 tablespoons rye bread crumbs

2 tablespoons prepared Dijon mustard

2 tablespoons strong Swedish mustard

2 tablespoons maple syrup

2 teaspoons cornstarch

1 teaspoon ground cloves

½ teaspoon salt

½ teaspoon pepper

Preheat oven to 400 degrees. Place ham in large baking pan. In mixing bowl, whisk together remaining ingredients. Smear paste all over ham. Bake for 15 minutes or until paste turns to golden crisp crust and ham is heated through. Slice and serve hot or at room temperature.

SERVES 8–12

# Oyster Stew

Louise Sim's recipe, contributed by Fay Leyden, Blaine, Minnesota

My stepdad's cousin married a woman that my mom adored. Louise was tall and fun, much like my mother, and she and her husband spent Christmas Eve with my mom and Jim. While Louise was not a Swede, her recipe is a beautiful and delicious addition to my *julbord*.

2 cups milk

½ cup heavy cream

¼ cup (½ stick) butter

1 pint oysters with their liquor

1 teaspoon salt

pepper

oyster crackers for serving

In a large saucepan, heat milk and cream to scalding. In a separate saucepan, melt butter; add oysters and liquor. Cook over medium-low heat until edges of oysters begin to curl. Add oyster mix to milk and cream. Season with salt and pepper and garnish with oyster crackers.

SERVES 4

# Charlotte Hansen

Charlotte met me at the door of her condominium dressed in a pink bathrobe. It was 1 PM and she apologized for having overslept as she had spent the previous night watching then Senator Barack Obama's appearance on David Letterman. Charlotte was a ninety-four-year-old night owl, pop culture enthusiast, and political junkie.

Both of Charlotte's parents were born in north Minneapolis, Minnesota. Her father's parents came from Sweden, and her mother's parents from Norway. They met in a butcher shop where her father worked.

Charlotte's mother cooked mostly Norwegian fare rather than Swedish. "My mother was the dominant one, but at Christmas, my father being in the butcher shop, we had what we called Christmas sausage. He was smart enough to not call it Swedish sausage so that it satisfied Scandinavians. You'd be interested to know at Speedy's over here they make it." Charlotte referred to Tim and Tom's Speedy Market, a small grocery store near her St. Anthony Park neighborhood. "My father wouldn't let us give it [the recipe] away until after he died." In fact, Charlotte's father continued to make the sausage until two years before his death at age one hundred.

Christmas sausage not only flaunts an inclusive title, it also doesn't have the pasty bulk of a Swedish potato version. A comparison of recipes explains the unique flavor of Charlotte's father's Christmas sausage. Swedish potato sausage is made of both pork and beef, spiced mainly with allspice and onions, and stuffed into large beef casings. It is prepared by boiling in water or broth. Christmas sausage combines beef and pork, contains a good bit of sugar, is spiced mainly with allspice and pepper, contains no onions, and is stuffed into smaller hog casings.

Celebrated on Charlotte's family table, the Christmas sausage also starred at holiday meals throughout Minneapolis. Her mother traded the sausage with neighbors to fill out the rest of their Christmas menu, bartering for such mainstays as lefse.

Charlotte grew up during the 1920s in north Minneapolis, a block from the Mississippi River. Although their Camden neighborhood was predominantly Scandinavian, Charlotte attended North High School, where a majority of students were Jewish.

Charlotte's father's reputation as an excellent butcher followed her to lunch. "The Jewish boys just loved the sandwiches I had. I said, 'Well, if you're going to have my sandwich, I have to have your sandwich.' I got kosher beef sandwiches from the Jewish boys, until my father discovered that I was having kosher!" Charlotte laughed and shook her head as she recalled, "I never told him about it, but he could smell it on my breath. He was displeased. I think he was worried that his daughter might marry a Jew. I felt very badly about that kind of a situation."

Charlotte's Christmases included meatballs with brown gravy, cookies, and lutfisk. When she was raising her own family, the menu changed slightly: "Christmas Eve we had sausage along with lutfisk. Until my sons married and their wives couldn't stand the scent of the lutfisk. We thought it was best to give up the lutfisk and keep the family."

A few years after Charlotte passed away, I interviewed two of her sons. Mark and Dave met me at the Scandinavian-style home where Dave lives with his wife, Karen. The brothers were anxious to share their memories of Christmases with Charlotte. Even those memories they

thought might not be flattering, I found to be a charming description of an amazing woman.

Dave always loved Christmas, especially the rituals of preparation and baking cookies. "By eighth grade, I remember baking the cookies by myself. I liked to get into the mood, and I really liked baking Christmas cookies." That year he baked many batches when his mom was out of the house, then wrapped them and hid them in his room so that he could give them as gifts. Charlotte found his stash and gave them away to her friends and colleagues. When family friends heard about the borrowed cookies, they gifted Dave with a copy of *Betty Crocker's Cooky Book*, a cookbook that Dave still owns.

In 1951 Charlotte, her husband Henry, and her father Harry Lindquist bought a Christmas tree farm, the first such tree farm in Minnesota. Hansen Tree Farm is just outside of Anoka and remains operational. A fourth generation of Hansens now works the farm. Visitors spend the day searching for their tree, warming up at the campfire, and enjoying Harry's Christmas sausage.

# Potato Sausage

From Charlotte Hansen's father, Harry Lindquist, formerly of Minneapolis, Minnesota

30 pounds boneless pork

30 pounds potatoes, peeled

4–5 onions

1 pound salt

½ cup ground pepper

½ cup plus
1 tablespoon allspice

6 ounces sugar

beef casings

Cut meat, potatoes, and onions to accommodate grinder, then grind. Add spices and mix thoroughly. Fill beef casings to desired lengths and tie with twine, leaving room for expansion during cooking. Prick in several places before cooking. Boil slowly for about 45 minutes.

**SERVES ABOUT 200**

# Swedish Sausage

Susan Swanson, Mahtowa, Minnesota

3 pounds pork shoulder, ground

1 ½ pounds blade steak beef, ground

1 pound russet or Yukon gold potatoes, peeled and cooked, then cut into cubes

2 teaspoons ground allspice

1 ½ teaspoons salt

1 teaspoon pepper

hog casings (optional)

Mix meats, potatoes, and spices very well and run through grinder. Use instructions provided by manufacturer to fill hog casings. Alternatively, form large patties.

The traditional cooking method for potato sausage is to place sausages in gently simmering water and cook, uncovered, until inserted thermometer reads 150 degrees. Alternatively, grill over indirect heat to same temperature.

**MAKES 18 SAUSAGES**

# Alternative Swedish Christmas *Sylta* (Cooked Pork in Brine)

Provided by Dr. Sagrid E. Edman, St. Paul, Minnesota, as created by her mother and father, Sagrid J. and Eric W. Edman of Jamestown, New York

"I don't remember when we started this Christmas tradition, but it was probably in the late fifties or early sixties when my mother worked full time and had a busy household to take care of. Somehow she and my dad came up with this recipe. Mom did not want to be bothered with all the chopping and cooking that was involved with real *rull sylta* or the chopped variety.

"We used pork butts for both summer barbecue and winter roasting because they are juicy and flavorful. So with my *mormor*'s help, they decided to try just the plain cooked pork. It was so good that all our friends wanted to know how to fix it. It became part of our regular Christmas menu. I brought a plate of the sliced "alternative" several years ago to the *smörgåsbord* of one of the Swedish groups I belong to at the Swedish Institute, and several of the "real Swedes" wanted the recipe. It is just as good in the summer for a picnic with potato salad."

 **NOTES FROM SAGRID:** Pork butts have more fat than a loin, but are juicier and very tasty. Most of the fat will cook out as it simmers and can be skimmed off the broth after it has cooled. If you intend to use the broth, skim off the grease and discard. The broth makes a great base for vegetable soup, or use it to cook potatoes and rutabagas for mashed *rutmos*

3–4 pounds boneless pork butt roast (Boston butt or shoulder)

freshly ground black pepper

ground allspice

1 medium white or yellow onion, chopped

salt for brining

Open or unroll roast and sprinkle the inside with pepper and allspice according to taste. Roll up and tie with string about every 2 inches to hold roast together during cooking.

Place the pork in a large pot and add enough water to barely cover. Add onion and bring to a boil. Do not add salt or any other seasonings. After water comes to a boil, reduce heat so it simmers gently. Skim off any dark scum that accumulates at the top of the pot in the first few minutes. Cover loosely, but not with a tight lid or it will boil over.

Continue cooking at low simmer for 2 ½ to 3 hours or until a fork goes into the meat easily and you can tear off a piece of meat from the end. Do not cook till it falls apart; you do not want shredded pork as for barbecue. Turn off the heat and leave the roast in the broth for a few hours till it has cooled. Refrigerate in the broth till the accumulated grease comes to the top and hardens (see notes page 184).

Fill a nonreactive (glass, enamel, or stainless steel) pot or bowl with enough water to cover the meat. Before you add the cooled pork, make a brine by adding enough salt so that an egg floats above the bottom of the pan (see tip). If the egg sinks to the bottom of the pan, add more salt. If you taste the brine, it will be quite salty. Stir the brine so the salt dissolves, then add the meat. Weigh down the meat with a plate or something heavy to submerge. Refrigerate in brine for at least 2 to 3 days before serving. It will keep for a week or two (if you don't eat it up!).

To serve, carve thin slices with a sharp knife and sprinkle each slice with vinegar and freshly ground black pepper. Serve cold or at room temperature with rye bread or *knäckebröd*.

**SERVES 8–12**

 **TIP:** For the brine, my *mormor* said that the egg should float toward the top, but I find that too salty.

# Swedish **Caramel Custard**

Adapted from Mrs. Otto Ecklund's recipe in *Friendship League's Book of Tested Recipes*

1 cup sugar

3 cups milk

4 eggs

salt

Preheat oven to 350 degrees. Add sugar in an even layer to heavy-bottomed stainless saucepan or skillet. Place over medium heat and use a silicone spatula or wooden spoon to gently move sugar from the edges of the pan to the center as it caramelizes and begins to brown. Do not stir vigorously. Sugar may melt unevenly. If lumps appear, lower heat and continue stirring until all sugar is liquefied. As sugar caramelizes, it will turn dark and amber and smell rich and nutty. When it just begins to smoke, remove from heat immediately and pour into 1 ½- to 2-quart baking dish. Pour milk into the already hot saucepan and bring to a boil.

In mixing bowl, whisk eggs and salt. Slowly whisk a cup of milk into the beaten eggs and continue whisking until well blended. Slowly pour egg-milk mixture into hot milk, whisking constantly. Pour mixture over the caramelized sugar; set pan inside a larger baking pan and fill outer pan with 1 inch water. Bake until just set, about 55 to 60 minutes. Chill flan for 2 hours or overnight. To serve, run a knife around edges and invert flan onto a large, rimmed serving platter (the syrup will flow over sides of the flan). Cut into wedges.

**SERVES 8**

# Lingonberry
# **Chiffon Cake**

My daughter's birthday is December 1. We begin our holidays by celebrating her. I created this chiffon cake in her honor. It has become a delicious addition to our *jul* dessert buffet.

You will need a stand mixer or a hand mixer and a very large bowl. Frost with 7-minute frosting or simple glaze of confectioner's sugar and lemon or orange juice. Garnish with lingonberries and additional lemon zest or candied lemons if desired.

1 cup plus 2 tablespoons cake flour

¾ cup sugar, divided

2 teaspoons baking powder

½ teaspoon salt

¼ cup vegetable oil

3 egg yolks plus 6 egg whites

⅓ cup plus 6 tablespoons vodka (or freshly squeezed orange juice for nonalcoholic cake)

1 teaspoon vanilla extract

zest of 1 lemon plus ⅓ cup lemon juice

¼ teaspoon cream of tartar

⅓ cup lingonberry preserves

Preheat oven to 325 degrees. Sift together flour, ½ cup sugar, baking powder, and salt. Set aside. In a large bowl, beat oil, yolks, 6 tablespoons vodka, vanilla, and lemon zest until smooth. Add flour to egg-oil mixture and beat until smooth and incorporated. Set aside.

In clean bowl beat egg whites and cream of tartar on low speed. As whites begin to foam, increase mixer speed and slowly add remaining ¼ cup sugar. Continue beating until whites are VERY stiff.

Whisk one-third of the beaten whites into flour-egg-oil mixture until well incorporated. Gently fold in remaining egg whites, taking care to keep whites airy. Pour batter into ungreased angel food cake pan and bake until inserted toothpick comes out clean, 45 to 50 minutes. Cool upside down in pan.

In small saucepan, whisk together lemon juice, lingonberry preserves, and remaining ⅓ cup vodka and place over medium-high heat. Whisk mixture until it comes to a gentle boil. Remove from heat and cool to room temperature.

Use wooden skewer to poke holes all over the exposed portion of cake. Pour half the syrup over cake. Set aside for 30 minutes. Remove cake from pan and place on serving plate. Poke holes in exposed top with wooden skewer and pour remaining syrup over cake. Frost and garnish as desired (see head note).

**SERVES 8**

# Ostkaka

Used by Bruce Karstadt's family for many years as dessert at Christmas Eve dinner. This recipe from Mrs. Carl Patrick was included in the *Measure for Pleasure* cookbook published in Lindsborg, Kansas, by the Bethany College Association.

---

*Ostkaka* (cheesecake) is a regional specialty in both Småland and Hälsingland, Sweden. The curd in *ostkaka* is separated from rich milk using rennet, which curdles the milk and separates the curd from the whey. The curds are then combined with sugar, flour, and flavoring and baked into a cake that is served just warm with berries.

Rennet can be purchased in tablet form at many co-ops, specialty groceries, and brewery supply stores. Store the tablets in your refrigerator, or freeze for up to three years.

8 ½ cups milk

½ cup flour

½ rennet tablet

2 eggs

½ cup sugar

1 cup half-and-half

½ teaspoon salt

1 teaspoon almond extract

lingonberries for serving

whipped cream for serving

Preheat oven to 300 degrees and grease 1 large (3-quart) or 2 smaller (1 ½–quart) baking dishes. Heat 8 cups milk to barely lukewarm (105 degrees); remove from heat.

Stir flour into remaining ½ cup milk and mix until smooth; add to the lukewarm milk and mix well. Dissolve the rennet in 1 tablespoon warm water. Mix this into the milk and let stand for about 10 minutes or until set. Do not stir. When set, cut the curd and let stand a few minutes until it separates. Pour off whey from time to time, or set mixture in a colander to drain. Beat eggs; stir in sugar, cream, salt, and almond extract, and mix into the curd.

Pour into prepared baking dish(es) and bake for about 1 ½ hours, until firm. Increase heat for final 10 minutes to brown top. Serve hot or cold with lingonberries or any other sweetened berries and top with whipped cream.

SERVES 8

# *Ostkaka* (Cheesecake)

Jane Sallstrom Grams's grandmothers Sigrid Monson and Ruth Sallstrom, Winthrop, Minnesota

"When my mother and her friends and relatives got together to make *ostkaka*, it was a big day. They would start by getting twenty gallons of milk from my dad's bulk tank, and then the fun began. They would bring their own casseroles to be filled. We still make this in smaller quantities. We like to serve this with homemade strawberry jam."

2 gallons milk

1 rennet tablet

1 cup flour

3 eggs, beaten

¾ cup sugar

1 ½ cups heavy cream

1 teaspoon salt

Preheat oven to 325 degrees and grease 2 baking dishes that will fit inside of large, high-sided pans. In a very large saucepan, warm milk over medium heat until lukewarm (about 105 degrees). Remove from heat.

Dissolve rennet tablet in 2 tablespoons warm water. Mix flour with a little warmed milk until smooth, and then stir into warm milk along with dissolved rennet. Stir until mixture curdles, then cover and let stand for 30 minutes. Use a large metal spoon to cut through mixture several times. Pour off the whey, or set mixture in a colander to drain.

In large mixing bowl, whisk together eggs, sugar, cream, and salt; stir into curd. Divide batter between prepared baking dishes. Place each dish inside a larger pan and add water to outer pan to half or three-quarters inner pan's height. Bake 1 ½ hours.

**SERVES 32**

# Quick *Ostkaka*

This recipe is not as curdy as traditional *ostkaka*, but the almonds add a delightful nutty crumb. To achieve a wetter curd, substitute drained cottage cheese for the ricotta.
Serve warm or at room temperature with vanilla-stewed berries or preserves and cream. Especially good with lingonberries.

½ cup slivered almonds

3 eggs

¼ cup flour

¼ cup sugar

¼ cup heavy cream

2 cups whole-milk ricotta

2 teaspoons almond extract

Preheat oven to 350 degrees and grease a pie plate. Pulse almonds in processor until mealy. Add remaining ingredients and process until smooth. Spread in prepared pan and bake for 45 minutes or until crust is light golden. Do not overbake.

SERVES 8

# Prune Bavarian Crème (Prune Whip)

Recipe by Ellida Viktoria Erickson Johnson, contributed by her
granddaughter Joann Lowrie, Becker, Minnesota

"I informed my brother, Dick, who hated the Prune Bavarian Crème, that his least favorite
food ever was going to be in a recipe book. He thinks there should be some sort of a
warning attached. Ever the comic.

"As a member of the American Swedish Institute as well as a volunteer facilitator at the
mansion AND the granddaughter of a Swedish immigrant who worked as a cook for a
wealthy family in Minneapolis, I would love to send you a Swedish holiday recipe! My
grandma emigrated from Sweden in 1902 and found employment with the H. B. Waite
family, who lived at 1325 Mount Curve Boulevard in Minneapolis. She told me stories of
the legendary meals that were served there and also showed me some of the handwritten
menus she had saved from that time: one that stands out in my mind was from December
3, 1909. It begins with 'caviare' and includes as a main course pheasant on a bed of wild
rice surrounded by a ring of peas and tomatoes! I'm thinking it must have looked like a
Christmas wreath on the serving platter . . . so creative! My grandma's Swedish holiday
meals (when she had a family of her own) were not as complex but I remember them
with such a happy heart! I did a scrapbook about her Christmas Eves for my daughter
and my two nieces a few years ago so that they could have a glimpse of a long-ago (1950s)
way to celebrate the holiday . . . two of her recipes are included in the scrapbook. One is
for Prune Bavarian Crème (which, I think, was my grandma's way of adding that touch of
elegance she encountered on Mount Curve to her Christmases) and one is for a pretty
common Swedish cookie . . . spritz."

½ cup cold water

2 envelopes unflavored gelatin powder

¾ cup sugar

½ teaspoon salt

1 ½ cups bottled prune juice

juice and zest of 2 lemons

2 cups stewed prunes, chopped very
fine, plus additional prunes for serving

1 ½ cups whipping cream, whipped,
plus more for serving

chopped pistachios for serving

Pour cold water in bowl and sprinkle gelatin
on top; add sugar, salt, and prune juice and
stir until gelatin is dissolved. Stir in lemon juice
and zest and chopped prunes and refrigerate.
When mixture begins to thicken, fold in
whipped cream. Turn into mold that has been
rinsed in cold water and refrigerate.

When firm, unmold and garnish with a big
dollop of whipped cream, halved prunes, and
chopped pistachio nuts. Decorate serving
platter with a sprig of holly!

SERVES 8

Attend a holiday *julbord* of mixed ethnicities (yes, the Norwegians and the Swedes can be friends) or hang around with a few Norwegians and you might be lucky enough to dabble in their holiday porridge tradition of *rømmegrøt*.

Beg hard enough and you might be so lucky as to have an expert in *rømmegrøt* make an entire batch for you, which is the spot where I found myself last year.

My friend Di LaChapelle is easily the World's Best *Rømmegrøt* Maker. I don't throw that title around lightly, and you can rest assured I've eaten more than any Swede's fair share of good *rømmegrøt*. Di is a *rømmegrøt* master. Armed with a pint of cream, a bit of flour, and a few cups of milk, she stirs and mashes the mixture into the smoothest, most buttery, creamy, rich concoction imaginable. On page 193 is her recipe, handed down through generations.

Di's family lovingly refers to the porridge as cream mush, an ironic name for a pudding fit for the Nordic gods. *Rømmegrøt* is magic.

# Rømmegrøt

As passed down from Jessie Jammer, formerly of Spring Valley, Wisconsin, to Anne Hammer, formerly of Baldwin, Wisconsin, to Diane LaChapelle, Stillwater, Minnesota

Flour amount varies according to humidity and age of the cream. Di uses Wondra because it comes sifted. The entire cooking process takes up to an hour, although larger batches take much longer.

2 cups heavy cream

⅓–⅔ cup sifted flour (see head note)

2 cups milk, hot

1–1½ tablespoons sugar

⅛ teaspoon salt

cinnamon for serving

Add cream to large skillet over medium-high heat. Add ⅓ cup flour and stir with flat wooden spoon or heatproof spatula, occasionally smashing any lumps against the side of the pan. Cook and stir until the mixture thickens and begins to become a consistent ball of batter.

Slowly sift in more flour and continue stirring and smashing. When butter begins to separate, stop adding flour. Stir constantly to prevent scorching and occasionally remove pan from the burner, adjusting heat, if any batter becomes hard and golden.

Use a metal spoon to remove separated butter; reserve for serving. Add hot milk to the batter, about ¼ cup at a time, stirring to mix well. When batter becomes a creamy pudding consistency, stir in sugar and salt. Taste and adjust seasoning if needed.

Divide pudding into serving dishes, float the butter on top of each, and garnish with a bit of sugar and cinnamon. Serve very warm but not hot (butter and sugar could burn).

**SERVES 6**

six
JUL

Swedish Christmas begins on Christmas Eve with visits from *tomte* (or Santa), and celebrations peak on Christmas Day.

Across Sweden just before Christmas, families, especially farm families, celebrated with *julhög* (Christmas pile). Historically, each member of the family was allotted their own *julhög*, meant to sustain them before holiday feasting began. The beautiful pyramids of breads and treats were decorative as well, and while the practice of *julhög* became less common, the Christmas pile is now a symbolic centerpiece in many homes.

To create your own *julhög*, begin with hardy fare on the bottom rungs. Rye crisp or *knäckbröd* makes a sturdy base. Top with a thin bread, then a miniature loaf of round rye or wheat bread. Next, place a soft, delicate cardamom roll, a sturdy slice of aged cheese, dried sausage, and a gingerbread cookie, all crowned with a perfect apple or orange. Decorate the edges of the *julhög* with shell-on hazelnuts, almonds, pecans, and walnuts, as well as dried fruits.

*Julhög* (page 195)

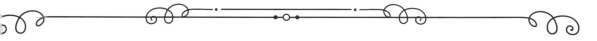

> On Christmas morning our stockings were so stuffed they actually burst and Santa had to leave larger gifts in piles beneath the sagging toes.

Presents spilled out from the Christmas tree across the entire living room floor. From the kitchen we could smell the almond from Mom's Danish, which took forever to bake on a morning when anticipation peaked and I was delirious with want.

Mom's recipe for Danish Puff came from Betty Crocker, but Betty wasn't the only, or even the first, to combine pie crust and cream puff pastry (choux dough) with almond extract and powdered sugar glaze. I came across recipes from countless old Scandinavian, church, and community cookbooks, as well as online versions providing no original references.

Called Danish Puff, Kringler, and a number of other names, this recipe belongs to many families as we wake up on Christmas morning ready to inhale the smells and flavors of Christmas Day.

**NOTE:** I've seen a Chicago rendition of this pastry that calls for whipping a few ounces of almond paste in the food processor, then beating it into the choux ball before adding the eggs. I've also made my own version using store-bought puff pastry instead of pie crust, and a thin layer of lingonberry preserves.

# Swedish **Kringle**, **Kringlor**, **Kringler**, or **Danish**

Susan Swanson

"This is best eaten the same day. AND it may look complicated but it is NOT . . . it is an almost foolproof recipe. I say that because one of my grandmothers and my mom didn't like to cook and these were their 'regulars' for celebrations. They look good and taste fabulous!"

**For the crust**

½ cup (1 stick) cold butter, cubed

1 cup flour

1 tablespoon ice water

¼–1 teaspoon almond extract

Preheat oven to 350 or 375 degrees. With a pastry blender or two knives, cut the butter into the flour until the size of small peas. Quickly stir in water just until dough can be formed into a ball. Wrap and refrigerate until ready to use. When filling is ready, pat dough onto a baking sheet in 2 long strips about 2 ½ to 3 inches wide.

**For the topping**

1 cup water

½ cup (1 stick) butter

1 cup flour

3 eggs

½–1 teaspoon almond extract

In saucepan, bring water and butter to boiling. Remove from heat and add flour all at once, beating until ball of smooth dough forms. Add eggs, one at a time, beating with a wooden spoon until each egg is completely incorporated into dough. Stir in extract. Spread over tops of the strips. Use wet fingers to evenly spread from edge to edge of the crust. Bake for 40 to 60 minutes, until golden brown and still slightly puffed.

**For the frosting**

1 cup confectioner's sugar

1–4 tablespoons butter, softened

½–1 teaspoon almond extract

evaporated milk, cream, or whole milk as needed

slivered almonds

In small mixing bowl, whisk together confectioner's sugar, butter, and almond extract. Add a little evaporated milk, cream, or whole milk to reach desired consistency. Use to frost cooled kringle. Garnish with slivered almonds.

SERVES 10

# Dopp i Grytan

Barbara Scottston, member of the Anoka County Historical
Society and formerly of Anoka, Minnesota

I am a second-generation Swedish American and grew up with the Christmas tradition of *dopp i gryta*. I expect the traditional story of its history remained preserved in my grandfather's telling. Perhaps the recipe was even preserved by its very isolation once in America. As with many immigrant cultures, traditions may have evolved (or even been abandoned) back in the Old Country but remained in a time warp here, as those immigrants strove to memorialize their rapidly fading past.

Fast-forward to the days when it was even abandoned by my family here. Grandparents were gone, and their daughter (my mother) had become a snowbird with an empty nest and a new husband. One Christmas, she was returning to Minnesota, and so to introduce my own children to a version of their Swedish heritage—but mostly to gift my mother a trip down Memory Lane—I re-created the Christmas Eve *dopp i gryta*. It was no small task researching the recipe in pre-internet days, but my memory served me well, and my mother endorsed the end product as authentic. Mothers are swell that way.

My grandfather's story was much more embellished than the explanation found on the internet today: just as a way to use up old, hard bread.

Gunnar Peterson (1889–1965) was born in Småland, Sweden. He immigrated to St. Paul, Minnesota, in 1906, and unlike many previous Swedish emigrants, poverty was not his motive to leave home. His family was financially secure, but he sought more diverse opportunities for his future than what he believed were available for his twelve siblings, who all remained in Sweden.

In 1910, he married Sigrid Carlson (1889–1956), who had arrived only two years earlier from her hometown of Jonköpping, Sweden. They were lifelong residents of St. Paul. She shared many cookie recipes with fel-

low members of the Ladies' Aid at Como Park Lutheran Church. Their three children didn't move very far away, and were usually together for holiday celebrations. This recollection is from their only granddaughter.

Gunnar remained in close connection with his family back in Sweden. It was clear he was brought up with strong roots of family pride, and he probably missed the customs of his natal family and homeland—which were not necessarily the same thing. To hear him tell it, the Christmas ritual of *dopp i grytan* belonged in every "good" Swedish household. Maybe it *was* widely practiced. Around 1900. In Småland. But his was one of the few Swedish American households still carrying it on in midcentury Minnesota. It became a bit of a novelty, as a parade of various nonfamily guests would be invited on Christmas Eve to partake in the experience. If this sounds as if it took on a life of its own, it did. However, he made sure that all were informed of its proper origins.

The meal was simply called "dup." The full name is translated to "dip-in-the-(stew)pot," a literal explanation of the meal as dipping a piece of bread into a pot of hot broth. Each Christmas Eve, the meal started with his story of it.

> *A long time ago, we Swedes didn't have the riches we all take for granted today. Times were harder, and there were no modern conveniences.* (Perhaps he'd interject a question to the children about how well their mothers would like to cook everything over a fire. Or some twist to keep the same old story interesting from year to year.) *Christmas was coming, and a lot of parents couldn't provide any gifts of even special food for their families at Christmas. But they really wanted to, and so they all worked very hard, and eventually things got better. After a long time, families were better off, and they started having nicer Christmases. But not yet as good as*

*what we have today. So when they were preparing the Christmas Day feast, and sharing good visits with all their friends and neighbors, they decided that they should take some time away from all this celebrating and remember their ancestors who lived in poverty and worked so hard to build up the good farms and homes that they were enjoying. So the day before glorious Christmas Day they would eat nothing, and in the afternoon they would break their fast by eating a poverty meal. You see, all they had were old crusts of bread and the broth they boiled down from animal bones. Not even any meat in their broth. That was eaten long ago. There was a long winter ahead, and this might be their main fare for a long time. So they would use their old, stale bread and soak up all the broth to the last drop, and be thankful for what they had.*

*And we should be thankful for what we have! Of course, we have all the good meat that today's dup broth was made from, and that will be served, too. But we will serve each plate with one slice of rye bread which has been soaked in the broth first. Then you may all enjoy the rest of the meal!*

And grace would be said. The dup broth sat in the middle of the table in a rather elaborate chafing dish, heated from below with a can of Sterno. The fire was present, if symbolic. Plates were passed up to the head of the table, and individual slices of proper limpa rye bread were floated in the broth and retrieved with a very wide spatula. There was a technique to this, so it was not to be left to the inexperienced. Fresh bread would deconstruct quickly in the hot broth, so a quick and deft hand was needed to plop an intact, but not-too-weeping slice of bread onto the dinner plate. Only logic, and the story, explained that dried-out crusts would be more suitable; he served the good bread.

Similarly, the meat was delectable. Hunks of pork loin, corned beef, and potato sausage. If many were seated around the table, there might be an extra serving bowl of meatballs in sour cream gravy. This

was a traditional Swedish dish, but unrelated to *dopp i gryta*. Just in case the "dup" menu was underappreciated, at least no one would go away hungry—even if that *was* the original point of the story. Nothing else was served. No potatoes, vegetables, or other festive Swedish foods. Beverages were beer and whiskey. Perhaps the traditional aquavit was never his personal favorite. The children got milk.

Dessert was more elaborate, as no Swede can ever serve just coffee. Platters of the traditional Christmas cookies, and flan—heavy baked custard with dark brown caramelized sugar sauce.

As with many immigrant cultures, traditions may have evolved (or even been abandoned) back in the Old Country but remained in a time warp here in America, as those immigrants strove to memorialize their rapidly fading past. Perhaps his traditional story of this Christmas Eve meal was historically preserved in his telling of it. Even the recipe may have been preserved by its very isolation in America. But it survives into the new millennium back in the homeland. At least one of Gunnar's nephews in Sweden carries on this Christmas Eve tradition to this day, and confirms that Gunnar correctly carried it to the New World. (However, today they use turkey broth.)

Eventually, the family abandoned it once both Gunnar and Sigrid were gone, and their own children became empty nesters and snowbirds for the holiday season. Grandchildren married into families with different traditions. Then one Christmas before the millennium turned, that one granddaughter attempted a replication of the tradition—both as a trip down Memory Lane and as an experience of Swedish heritage for the next generation of children around the Christmas Eve table. Research and memory resulted in this updated recipe for "dup."

Aquavit-Cured Gravlax (page 168), *Rårakor* (page 216), and Rye-Dill Blini (page 217)

*Dopp i Grytan*

# Dopp i Grytan

Barbara Scottston, formerly of Anoka, Minnesota

"Original recipe used pork loin, but this is too pricy for soup stock.
The ribs are an economical substitute."

2 tablespoons vegetable oil

2 pounds pork country ribs

2 pounds corned beef

1 tablespoon pickling spice

12 whole allspice berries

2 bay leaves

1 clove garlic

salt and pepper

1–2 rings potato sausage

limpa slices

Heat oil in a large stockpot and sear ribs for about 15 minutes, turning as needed to brown sides. Add corned beef and cover with enough water to make soup. Place pickling spice, allspice, bay leaves, and garlic in a tea infuser or cheesecloth bag and add to pot. Reduce heat to low so that the liquid is at a very gentle simmer. Cook, uncovered, for several hours, until meat is tender. Liquid should reduce, but add water if too much liquid evaporates. When meat is cooked, remove meat and seasonings from stock. Add salt and pepper to stock to taste.

About an hour before serving, slice potato sausage and add to the stock. Slowly boil the sausage until cooked, about 20 to 30 minutes. Debone the pork, cut beef into serving-size pieces, and heat before serving. Remove sausage chunks from the stock and add to the meat platter.

Serve the soup stock from a large chafing-style dish—with heat source below and wide opening at top—in the center of the table. Briefly float a piece of Swedish limpa rye bread in the broth until it soaks up broth but does not fall apart. Scoop it out with a large spatula that will support the bread slice as it is transferred to the diner's plate. Usually one person does the soaking/serving, and dinner plates are passed around the table. The meat is passed separately on a serving platter.

**SERVES 12**

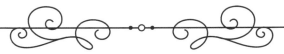

I winced at the thought of salting then boiling six pounds of relatively expensive roasts, but I was intrigued by the charming lore behind *dopp i gryta*.

In years when busy farm wives spent weeks preparing for the Christmas feast, *dopp* was a way to feed large families during the holidays without taking away from holiday kitchen tasks leading up to a bursting *julbord*. Stale slices of fennel- and caraway-scented limpa were added to the stew for flavor (and presumably to use up the bread).

My butcher set aside a ham cut pork (loin) and a London broil for this dish. I packed each roast in salt inside of a sturdy sealable plastic bag. Within twelve hours, the salt was already drawing moisture from each meat slab, and I carefully cradled each Baggie of meat and liquid into a bowl in case of a leak.

Christmas Eve morning I placed the roasts in the bottom of my largest stockpot (it wasn't big enough, and eventually I transferred the stew into my canning pot) with the water and seasonings. After a three-hour simmer, the meat temperature was 170 degrees. I removed the pot from heat and cooled it for an hour and a half before covering the pot with foil and setting it out in our cold garage. (Food safety rules call for soups and stews to reach 70 degrees within two hours before setting the pot in a cool place. If your stew doesn't cool quickly enough, use an ice bath.)

Christmas Day I transferred the stew and three loaves of limpa bread to my mom's house, where my family was ready and willing to taste the *dopp*. I sliced the meat into serving portions, offering bites to family members who had gathered in the kitchen. The meat was salty but flavorful, with a hint of allspice. I placed the sliced meat back in the stock and simmered the stew for another hour or two while our meatballs and Janssons cooked.

This recipe makes a beautiful bowl of stew, with a clear but flavorful stock and tender bites of roast.

# Dopp i Grytan

Recipe from Albertha Sundstrom, Bruce Karstadt's grandmother,
published in *Measure for Pleasure* in Lindsborg, Kansas

"This was served each Christmas Eve day at twelve noon as a lunch for family and
friends. We would sit down and eat *dopp* and bread, then cookies, and divinity. I loved
getting together for *dopp* at Christmas Eve at noon at my grandmother's house.
That was special."

⊁ ⊰

up to 1 cup salt

3 pounds veal or lean beef

3 pounds lean pork

8 black peppercorns

10 allspice berries

2 bay leaves

stale slices

Salt meat generously, place in resealable plastic
bags, and put in refrigerator for 2 to 3 days.

The day before serving, rinse roasts well
with cold water, place in a large kettle, and
cover with water (about 8 quarts), adding
peppercorns, allspice, and bay leaves. Bring
to a gentle boil, reduce heat, and simmer,
uncovered, for 3 hours, replenishing water
as it evaporates. Remove from heat and
cool 1 to 2 hours. Cover and place pot in
a cold place overnight. (A cold Minnesota
garage works well.)

In the morning, skim off fat and cut meat into
serving pieces, returning them to the pot.
Place stockpot on stove and boil slowly until
noon. Serve with rye bread (stale limpa is best).
This may be served in soup bowls. Some like
the broth and meat poured over the bread;
others prefer eating bread and butter with
their soup. Pickles, coffee, and cookies are
good accompaniments.

The soup is extremely nutritious, and you
will find you will need no more food until the
Christmas Eve dinner is served.

**SERVES 15**

# Palt

## SCOT PEARSON

At Norsk Høstfest, an event in Minot, North Dakota, that bills itself as North America's largest Scandinavian festival, they bring me in as the Swedish American food representative. I trot out onto the Nordic Kitchen stage twice a day to educate, entertain, and feed the masses. In between demonstrations I mingle with Vikings and trolls and eat a lot of white food. Not a bad gig.

My friend Scot recently returned to Minot after living a few years in Minneapolis. During my second *Høstfest* tour he invited me to his home, where he and his sister Lori treated me to their family's version of *palt*.

While I've enjoyed *kroppkakor* (golf ball– to baseball-sized potato dumplings with a pork center), until I tasted Scot's version I'd never seen let alone tasted *palt*. *Palt* is made from ground raw potatoes and flour, filled with pork belly or salt pork, and served with melted butter and lingonberries. The size of a softball, *palt* makes its *kroppkakor* sibling look downright dainty.

Scot warned me prior to my visit, "We don't have any real recipe for it; it's one of those family things that we learned if we were interested, and we participated in the making of it. It is sort of like riding a bicycle to us."

When I arrived at Scot's place, he ushered me into his kitchen, where a large pot of water was already boiling and his sister Lori was peering into a hefty ceramic dish filled with white dough. Scot handed me a glass of Dom Pérignon (the pairing of choice for any *palt* aficionado) and dunked his fingers into a bowl of water, generously wetting both hands before using them to dip into the dough and form a gooey

softball-sized orb. He explained that the dough must be wet enough to be pliable, but not so wet that it runs through your fingers. Pretty technical stuff. He eyeballed a few tablespoons of flour and mixed it into the dough, then attempted to form another globe. This time he was satisfied, and he began to deftly roll the dough around a good bit of ground pork. "This is uncured pork. The salt pork looked kind of gray, so this was the better choice."

Lori nodded her approval as Scot showed his formed dumpling. He brought a wide ladle to the pot of heavily salted boiling water and scooped a bit of the water into the ladle before adding the dumpling and lowering it into the bath. I sipped my champagne while Scot and Lori had an intense conversation about how the dumplings sink, then float, then sink again before they are completely cooked. "It takes about an hour and a half," Scot told me.

When it was my turn to form a dumpling, I mimicked Scot's movements. "How much pork do I add?"

"I usually start out worried that I won't have enough pork to make all of the *palt*, but by the end of the process I've got extra meat. Don't be afraid to add a generous amount," Scot said. I shoved about a quarter cup of pink meat into the dumpling and attempted to form a ball around the pork. An hour later when we retrieved the completed dumplings, one had exploded, and Scot and Lori were kind enough not to accuse me of being responsible for the ill-formed *palt*, although we all knew I was.

The Pearsons enjoyed *palt* at all of their special gatherings, including Christmas. Scot and Lori agreed it made them feel connected

to their extended family, especially when they were growing up in California, far from grandparents and cousins who lived in the Dakotas. "The other things I grew up with were more along the lines of the *krumkake* and kringler. Lori and I are the two that have really run with the Scandinavian heritage thing and have done Swedish *smörgåsbord*-type Christmas Eve dinners for our families, off and on. We have made things such as Jansson's temptation, potato sausage, pickled red cabbage, Swedish limpa bread, pickled herring, and quite a number of other things. We normally just do some Google researching and come up with our list and then get together and whip things up." Scot continued with his family's history:

> My grandfather, Arvid (Persson, originally) Pearson, emigrated from Sweden in 1910, at the age of about fifteen-sixteen. He was the youngest of thirteen children, and his mother had died (sadly by suicide, after finding out that her husband had a mistress) some years earlier and his father had married his mistress. . . . But he traveled by ship from Sweden to the USA, and his next elder sister traveled along with him, though she died on the ship. But he had three or four elder siblings that had already emigrated and were living in South Dakota, so he made his way there.

> He worked for a variety of farmers and used to see this beautiful young lady walking along the country road every late afternoon, and she would wave at him out in the field before disappearing down the farm driveway, across the road.

> In time, this young lady began coming back out with cold water and a sandwich for this young Swedish farmhand and they became sort of acquainted. Her name was Laura Page, and she was a young schoolteacher and was boarding with the Shonstad family there. They fell for one another, and the rest is a beautiful history of which I've been so blessed to be a part of.

> Laura Dorothy Page Pearson was probably the nearest thing to an angel on earth that I ever have come across. I named my only daughter after her. She was the most genuinely loving, kind, and gentle-hearted person and an incredible cook and housekeeper. I've

spent my life looking around and buying odds and ends that are similar to things that they had in their home. Even my house reminds me so much of theirs, as did the one I bought in Minneapolis. I've got a full collection of dinnerware that dates back to the late 1950s or earlier 1960s, just like they had when I was a child, and whenever we make this *palt*, I insist that we eat it on those. I'm a goof—but a sentimental one, and I'm sure there could be worse things to be.

My grandmother was not Swedish, so her cooking was quite a variety of things, and she did make some of the Swedish things, too, including the *palt*, kringler, ginger cookies, limpa bread, and so forth. I don't have my own recipes for many of those things, though I do for limpa bread. The recipe that I've got for that is award-winning: orange zest, anise, fennel, and caraway seeds broken to bits in a Ziploc bag with a hammer; plus brown sugar and molasses. It's intense, moist, and so good with some cool butter on it.

Back in the 1980s, even before we moved here to Minot (this was my wife's hometown), I spotted this house. It was nothing fancy at all, but it reminded me so much of the house that my Pearson grandparents bought in 1946 and they lived in until they could no longer be on their own and had to go into the nursing home. I had admired this house always and used to tell my ex-wife that if it ever were to go up for sale, to beware because I would probably want to buy it, even to have as a rental. In the early part of May, I was on my way home from a day's work at my son's office and made my way up through this older part of Minot, as I so often did. I came to the corner of Second Street and Fourteenth Avenue and glanced the direction of the old house that I always loved and spotted the FOR SALE sign out in front. I sat and stared in disbelief. I rushed on home to look it up on the internet. Sure enough: it had just gone onto the market. I couldn't believe how reasonably priced it was, and I called a former patient of mine, from years ago, who's a realtor here, and I set up an appointment to look. I immediately loved it, made an offer, and here I am. It's not as roomy as my south Minneapolis house was, but it's of the same era and has a lot of the similar charm that the houses from the 1920s have. I'm so happy to be here. It's a work in progress, but then aren't they all . . . and aren't we all?

It's a fun process and I consider it a festivity.

We sat down in Scot's dining room. The table was set with the china plates, serving dishes, and glasses similar to those that belonged to his grandmother. Scot said a prayer of thanks, and we began our meal.

We each lifted a heavy dumpling onto our plates, and I followed Lori and Scot's instructions to "Cut a window into the top of the *palt*," and added a few tablespoons of good butter to the opening. "*Palt* is just a vehicle for the butter," Scot and Lori explained. Salt and pepper and, for me, lingonberries completed the dish.

The dumplings were dense and starchy. Scot made a joke about wallpaper paste, but I waved off his remarks. The *palt* were almost silky, and the sweet-tart lingon and pork paired off like an old Swedish love story.

As the pat of butter melted down into the white crevices of potato dumpling and mingled with my generous lumps of lingon, I understood. This simple, humble swell of potato celebrated the history of Scot and Lori, of their family, and of every meal eaten with someone missing.

My glass of champagne was not yet empty, but there was a large tumbler of milk next to my plate. "You have to drink milk with *palt*. It is the law," Lori told me. I followed her orders.

I gulped down the milk and felt a communion with the entire Pearson clan.

# Palt

It can take 30 to 45 minutes to shape the dough before placing balls in their comfy, slow-simmering water, depending on the dexterity and number of kitchen helpers.

5 pounds russet or other low-starch baking potatoes

5 pounds flour

salt

8–12 ounces uncured pork or salt pork, ground

butter, pepper, and lingonberries for serving

heavy cream or half-and-half for leftovers (optional)

Bring large pot of water to boil; add several tablespoons of salt per gallon of water. Lower heat so that water is just simmering; cover pot with a lid.

Peel and grind the potatoes. Use a sturdy spoon to mix in flour, a few cups at a time, until a loose dough forms. Season generously with salt. Dough should be firm enough to hold a ball shape in wet hands, but not so firm as to hold its shape on its own.

With very wet hands, form softball–sized ball, insert 2 tablespoons pork into center of dough, and shape dough around pork to make an orb. Working quickly, dip a wide ladle into pot of simmering water, carefully drop dough ball into spoon, and lower into simmering water. If water stops simmering, increase heat. Continue adding dough balls into bath and adjusting heat to low simmer. Use ladle to ease any balls away from sticking to the bottom of the pot. When all dumplings are in the water, cover pot with lid and watch carefully to keep water at a low simmer. Do not boil. Simmer, covered, for 90 minutes.

Remove dumplings with a slotted spoon and serve hot with lots of salt, pepper, and butter, and lingonberry preserves if desired.

Chill leftovers. Slice into ¾-inch pieces and place in skillet with a few tablespoons of butter. Fry until dumplings are just golden. Add enough cream or half-and-half to barely cover the dumplings and bring to a simmer. Cook the cream sauce until it thickens. Serve hot.

**MAKES 10–12 DUMPLINGS**

There are a variety of Swedish potato dumplings, including *klimp* (small dumplings usually added to stew or soup), *kroppkakor* (golf ball– to tennis ball–sized dumplings typically made with potatoes, all-purpose flour, salt, water, and cream and occasionally eggs), and *palt* (softball sized).

Variations of *kroppkakor* contain pork blood, sugar, and rye flour. Others use raw potatoes rather than cooked (there is also a version that combines both cooked and raw), but *kroppkakor* made with raw potatoes are said to turn blue once cooked. Therefore, I stick to recipes that call for cooked potatoes.

Both *kroppkakor* and *palt* commonly contain a center of suet or salt pork and are cooked by simmering in either heavily salted water or ham hock broth. Starchy potatoes should not be used for any variation of these dumplings, as the dough becomes a pasty mess. Stick to a russet or other baking type of potato.

The word *kroppkakor* translates as "body cakes," referring either to how the dumpling fills the eater or to the size of the dumplings.

Swedish dumplings are not for the faint of heart. In an attempt to lighten them up I added cream cheese (you could also use ricotta) and panko to the recipe and made each ball about half the size of traditional *kroppkakor*. A warning: a little *kropp* goes a long way. Serve with lots of lingonberries, butter, and any leftover filling. These are also good with white gravy or a wine reduction.

# Potato Dumplings (*Kroppkakor*)

3–4 cups russet potatoes, cooked and pushed through ricer

3 tablespoons cream cheese

2 egg yolks

½ teaspoon freshly grated nutmeg, divided

½ cup flour

½ cup panko bread crumbs

6 slices thick-cut bacon, chopped

½ white onion, chopped

¼ teaspoon allspice

¼ teaspoon pepper

melted butter and lingonberries for serving

In a very large mixing bowl, stir together potatoes, cream cheese, yolks, and ¼ teaspoon nutmeg. Gradually stir in flour and panko until the dough is soft and pulls away from the sides of the bowl. Chill 30 minutes.

Over medium-high heat, fry bacon until it is just beginning to crisp. Drain fat and reserve.

Add onions to bacon and cook until bacon is crisp and onions are soft, about 8 minutes. Season with remaining ¼ teaspoon nutmeg, allspice, and pepper.

Roll dumplings into balls of about 2 tablespoons each (use a small ice cream scoop for ease). Gently press middle of ball and fill with a bit of the bacon and onion mixture. Close ball around mixture and roll out any seams. Gently press to slightly flatten. Place dumplings on floured parchment paper.

Bring a large pot of salted water to boil. Working in batches, carefully slip dumplings into boiling water. When dumplings float to surface, cook an additional 3 minutes. Using slotted spoon, remove from pot and transfer to plate.

In a clean pan, melt reserved bacon fat. Fry dumplings about 1 minute each side or until golden. Serve warm with melted butter and lingonberries or with gravy.

**MAKES 30 DUMPLINGS**

# *Rårakor*
## (Swedish Potato Pancakes)

I am superstitious when it comes to New Year's Eve. Whatever mood I am in that evening seems to intrude on the rest of the year. But I never allow that mood to change the first meal of the year. In my house, the New Year (and my hands) always smell like fresh-squeezed tangerines that I add to champagne that I drink while frying platters of rye-dill blini and Swedish potato pancakes. We top the blini and the potatoes with crème fraîche, aquavit-kissed gravlax (leftover from Christmas celebrations), and inexpensive roe. For a sweet ending, lingonberries and maple syrup crown the blini, and we gulp down good, hot coffee.

For sweeter cakes, serve with sour cream, applesauce, or lingonberries; for savory cakes, add a tablespoon each of minced chives and dill to batter before frying and serve with sour cream, caviar, chives, and gravlax.

2 Yukon Gold potatoes, shredded and squeezed dry

¼ cup grated white or yellow onion

2 eggs

2 tablespoons flour

salt and pepper

olive oil and butter

Stir together potatoes, onions, eggs, and flour; season with salt and pepper. In a large skillet, melt 2 teaspoons each of butter and olive oil over medium heat. Fry small round clumps of potato mixture, about 2 tablespoons per round, in butter/oil about 5 minutes each side or until golden brown. Place completed cakes on paper towels in warm oven until ready to serve.

**MAKES ABOUT 24 CAKES**

# Rye-Dill **Blini**

Top with crème fraîche, gravlax, and roe. Garnish with fresh dill and chives.

1 teaspoon yeast

3 tablespoons warm water

1 tablespoon sugar

1 cup milk

2 eggs, separated

½ cup medium (not coarse) rye flour

½ cup all-purpose flour

pinch salt

2 tablespoons butter, melted

2 tablespoons finely chopped fresh dill

In small bowl, stir together yeast, water, and sugar and set aside until foamy, about 5 minutes. In large mixing bowl, whisk together yeast mixture, milk, egg yolks, flours, and salt; cover and let rise for 1 hour.

Beat egg whites to stiff peaks. Fold whites into batter. Stir in melted butter and dill; set aside 10 minutes.

Place nonstick skillet over medium heat. Working in small batches, drop 1 to 2 tablespoons of batter onto skillet for each pancake. Cook 1 to 2 minutes; flip when bubbles appear on surface of each cake, and continue cooking additional 30 to 60 seconds. Cover cooked blini to keep warm until serving.

**MAKES ABOUT 24 (2-INCH) CAKES**

# Cardamom Toast Ice Cream
## with Lingonberry Jam

Stephanie Lawrence, Minneapolis, Minnesota

I met Stephanie when she was a student in a few of my Nordic cooking classes at the American Swedish Institute. Stephanie is one of those women who accepts recipes with gratitude, then lets it slip that she is working on a peach-basil shrub or an amazing bread I've never heard of. She is one of those undercover remarkable cooks whose humility masks her creative abilities.

Stephanie mentioned this ice cream during class one night as we were discussing ways to repurpose leftover Christmas cookies and breads. Stephanie toasts stale *pulla* (Finnish cardamom bread) and blends it into an ice cream batter adapted from Jeni Britton Bauer's *Jeni's Splendid Ice Creams at Home*.

2 cups milk

1 tablespoon plus 1 teaspoon cornstarch

1 ½ ounces (3 tablespoons) cream cheese, softened

⅛ teaspoon fine sea salt

½ teaspoon cardamom extract

1 ¼ cups heavy cream (preferably not ultra-pasteurized)

⅔ cup sugar

2 tablespoons light corn syrup (not high-fructose) or tapioca syrup

3 (¾-inch thick) slices *pulla* or other cardamom or cinnamon bread

1 tablespoon butter, melted

⅓–½ cup lingonberry preserves

Mix about 2 tablespoons of the milk with the cornstarch in a small bowl to make a smooth slurry. Whisk the cream cheese and salt together in a medium bowl until smooth. Fill a large bowl with ice.

Combine the remaining milk, cardamom extract, cream, sugar, and corn syrup in a 4-quart saucepan, bring to a rolling boil over medium-high heat, and boil for 4 minutes. Remove from heat and gradually whisk in the cornstarch slurry. Return the mixture to a boil over medium-high heat and cook, stirring, until the mixture is slightly thickened, about 1 minute. Remove from heat.

Gradually whisk the hot milk mixture into the cream cheese until smooth. Pour the mixture into a 1-gallon plastic freezer bag and submerge sealed bag in the ice bath. Let stand until cold, about 30 minutes.

Preheat oven to 250 degrees and line a baking sheet with parchment paper. Place pulla on sheet and bake until the bread is dry throughout, about 15 minutes. Use a food processor or blender to crumb the bread while adding melted butter.

Pour chilled ice cream base into the frozen ice cream maker canister. Spin until thick and creamy. Pour in the toast crumbs during the last 5 minutes of the process, evenly distributing throughout.

Pack the ice cream into a storage container beginning with a few dollops of lingonberry preserves randomly dispersed in the bottom of the container. Then dollop some ice cream on top (don't swirl!), followed by more dollops of preserves, then ice cream, and so on, ending with a few lingonberry preserve dollops on top. Press a sheet of parchment paper directly against the surface, and seal with an airtight lid. Freeze until firm, at least 4 hours.

SERVES 8

*seven*

# TWELVE DAYS OF JUL: THE REVELRY CONTINUES

# While being an American

was the aim of most Swedish immigrants in 1900, there were organizations within urban communities where Swedish cultural identity continued to flourish. Swedish costumes, language, and food were retained on the Swedish stage, in the Swedish press, and in churches and hospitals. Additionally, saloons became a social hub where immigrant men gathered to exchange job information; eventually those saloons became a hotbed for labor organization. Women organized in church kitchens, where prohibition became a church mission. The temperance movement was a useful tool in the attempt to shut down unions. Temperance champions and anti-unionists became partners in the kitchen.

The temperance movement was also popular among Swedish immigrants who eschewed not only drunkenness but alcohol in general. Leaders of temperance included Swan Turnblad, who made millions from his publishing empire, including a Swedish-language newspaper that advocated the cause. *Svenska Amerikanska Posten* (The Swedish American Post) was the largest Swedish newspaper in America, and the money it earned helped Turnblad build an imposing residence on Park Avenue in Minneapolis. He donated the house to establish the American Swedish Institute, which continues to function today as a museum and gathering place that promotes enduring links to Sweden through culture, migration, the environment, and the arts—a hefty inheritance from a newspaper built on temperance.

# Bruce's Best *Glögg*

Bruce Karstadt, Minneapolis, Minnesota

Use the cheapest wines possible, as the spices will overwhelm any flavors.

1 (1.5-liter) bottle Merlot or Cabernet wine

1 (750-milliliter) bottle tawny port

1 cup sugar

2 cinnamon sticks

1 cup raisins

peel of 1 orange

24 whole cloves

18 cardamom seeds, crushed

1 piece crystallized or fresh ginger

1 cup orange-flavored vodka

Warm the wines with the sugar, cinnamon sticks, raisins, and orange peel. Place the cloves, cardamom seeds, and ginger in a cheesecloth bag and add to the pot. Warm until near boiling. Remove the spices and orange peel but not the raisins. Stir in vodka. Serve immediately or bottle and serve another day.

SERVES 12

# Gloria Hawkinson's Dad's *Glögg*

1 cup sugar

1 gallon port wine

1 quart alcohol (brandy, rum, vodka)

1 cup prunes

1 cup apricots

Add sugar to a large pot. Heat until caramelized (see method page 186), then stir in remaining ingredients. Do not boil after adding alcohol, but keep *glögg* just below a simmer and serve hot.

**SERVES 32–40**

**OPTIONAL:** Light a match to alcohol, then cover to put out flame.

# White *Glögg*

1 (750 milliliter) bottle dry white wine

½ cup citron aquavit

¼ cup sugar

1 tangerine, sliced

1 bay leaf

1 cinnamon stick

1 star anise

thumb-sized piece fresh ginger, peeled and chopped

freshly grated nutmeg

Warm wine, aquavit, sugar, tangerine, bay leaf, cinnamon, anise, and ginger over medium-high heat until sugar just dissolves. Do not simmer. Move to *glögg* pot and keep heated. Serve in mugs with sprinkle of nutmeg.

**SERVES 8–12**

# Glögg

Gustavus Adolphus College, St. Peter, Minnesota

"The homey scent of heavily spiced spirits fills the holiday air. Sip a warm cup of *glögg* served with crispy *pepparkakor* (Swedish ginger cookies, pages 63–64), and share the Christmas cheer!"

1 (750 milliliter) bottle dry red wine

1 cup aquavit or quality vodka

⅓ cup granulated sugar

⅓ cup packed brown sugar

peel and juice of 1 orange

2 tablespoons lemon juice

6 cinnamon sticks, broken

6 whole cloves

2 tablespoons candied ginger

4 cardamom pods, shells removed, seeds lightly crushed

24 golden raisins

24 raisins

12 whole blanched almonds

In large saucepan, stir together the wine, aquavit, sugars, orange peel, juices, cinnamon, cloves, ginger, and crushed cardamom seeds. Heat to simmer for 15 minutes; taste and adjust sweetness if additional sugar is needed. Do not boil.

Strain the *glögg* through a fine-mesh sieve into a candle-warmed copper kettle and keep warm. Place 2 of each of the raisins and 1 of the almonds in each of 12 *glögg* cups or teacups. Fill with *glögg* and sip. Small spoons help scoop out the raisins and almond.

SERVES 12

# Canute
# KNUT DAY

Across Sweden, *Tjugondag Knut* (Twentieth Day Knut, or twenty days following Christmas) marks the official end of Christmas. The day is named for St. Canute (Knut in Swedish), a Danish duke who was killed on January 7, close enough to the Epiphany on January 6 that the two days began to morph, which begat a Christmas theme to Knut. Eventually St. Knut's day moved to January 13.

The main event on *Tjugondag Knut*, also known as *julgransplundring* (Christmas tree plundering), is clearing the house of all things *jul*, as well as a final feast of Christmas leftovers that includes any candy and cookies remaining on the decorated Christmas tree. The tree is tossed, and Christmas is over.

Bruce Karstadt, president and CEO of the American Swedish Institute in Minneapolis, Minnesota, sat across from me at *Fika*, the Nordic-inspired café that tempts ASI guests with pastries and *smörgåsar*. Piled on the table next to our sausage and shrimp was an assortment of precious old cookbooks from Bruce's collection.

They were the best kind, mostly community and church cookbooks with occasional smears of unidentified (presumably edible) stains and pages penciled with useful notes from the cooks who first owned them.

Bruce opened a thin spiral notebook that had belonged to his mother. In it were dozens of recipes and a coordinating menu written in Patty Karstadt's neat cursive. "My mom's cousin Charlotte in Dallas always had a Canute *smörgåsbord*. My mom began to do her own version of the smorgasbord in January." Bruce added that his mom's Canute dinner parties included thirty-five to forty guests. The menu listed food enough for a feast, with a few items crossed off the menu to make way for obvious new additions.

While Patty's mom's Glug didn't make an appearance on the Knut *smörgåsbord* menu, the raisin-based drink (made with grain alcohol) might provide some of us with motivation to plunder. ✐

# Glug

Potentia (Tensa) Swanson and Christine Larson, best friends from Lindsborg, Kansas; Tensa was Bruce Karstadt's maternal great-grandmother

| | |
|---|---|
| 4 cups water | Stir together water, raisins, cloves, and cinnamon. Simmer 1 hour, then strain. Cool mixture a bit, then pour in alcohol. Use a match to light and burn for 2 seconds. Add almonds and sweeten with brown sugar to taste. Serve warm. |
| 1 pound raisins | |
| 10 whole cloves | |
| 1 cinnamon stick | |
| 2 cups alcohol (brandy, rum, vodka) | |
| almonds for serving | |
| brown sugar for serving | |

**SERVES 8**

Glug (page 227) and Aquavit

# Aquavit

Marilyn Jensen Calkins, Rochester, Minnesota

Minot, North Dakota's Norsk Høstfest is billed as North America's largest Scandinavian festival. *Høstfest* is where we lovers of all things Nordic gather every autumn to celebrate Nordic-ness with music, dance, laughter, shopping, and food. I've been invited a few times to be the Swedish representative on the food stage, where twice a day I cook something sort of Swedish and talk to the masses about meatballs and *Flygande Jakob*, a hot dish of chicken, bananas, whipped cream, and Heinz chili sauce, topped with bacon and peanuts.

I'd just finished a demo on the Nordic Kitchen stage and was cleaning up when a friendly couple approached me. Marilyn introduced herself and started telling me about her aquavit. "You make it from scratch?" I asked.

Marilyn's husband nodded proudly and told me how the bottle of vodka steeping in caraway gets turned every time Marilyn walks by it. "You've got to keep turning it!" he explained.

3 teaspoons sugar

3 teaspoons caraway seeds

1 (1.75-liter) bottle inexpensive charcoal-filtered vodka

Add sugar and caraway to vodka in bottle. Place on counter and roll or shake every day for 3 days or until vodka tastes "right." Strain seeds (add them to a pork roast or country ribs) and store aquavit in freezer.

**MAKES 1.75 LITERS**

# Aquavit **Sidecar**

Mike McCarron started making a dill-flavored aquavit when he returned from Scandinavia and couldn't find any imported varieties of his favorite blend. His Gamle Ode aquavits are distilled at the 45th Parallel Distillery in New Richmond, Wisconsin, and, lucky for me, distributed throughout the heartland. In addition to a dill aquavit, Mike produces holiday, celebration, and rye blends. I've always got a stash of Mike's aquavit in my freezer, and it is fun to play bartender for family and friends who have yet to be introduced to the diverse flavors of caraway-scented spirits.

I've experimented with a variety of aquavits to make a Scandinavian version of a sidecar. Gamle Ode Celebration is my favorite, although you'll have success with Norwegian Linie or any aquavit with the traditional flavors of caraway, juniper, coriander, and anise.

Think of aquavit as a caraway-flavored vodka, similar to how we view gin as a juniper-flavored vodka.

2 ounces aquavit

¾ ounce Tattersall Orange Crema (or other orange liqueur, such as Cointreau)

¾ ounce lemon juice

confectioner's sugar

Pour liquids into shaker with lots of ice. Shake at least 50 times and pour into cocktail glass lined with confectioner's sugar. Garnish with lemon or orange twist.

SERVES 1

> I envy my friends who were born with a rolling pin in one hand and their great-grandma's lefse recipe in the other. I envy those huddled masses in Lutheran church basements where Norwegian grandmothers bestow upon them secrets of making the perfect lefse.

Sure, in my youth I dated quite a few Norwegians. It is difficult to avoid them in these parts. Yet it wasn't until I had the good sense to marry one that I began to dabble in the art of lefse making.

Lefse is that gorgeous, delicate, delicious Norwegian potato flatbread specialty, but Swedish Americans have been eating this bread for generations. Never having had a kindly Norwegian grandmother to guide me, I decided to take matters into my own hands, and now my friends and our children (and their friends) meet before Christmas every year for a day of lefse making. While I have not mastered the ball-roll-transfer-flip technique so vital in potato flatbread preparation, I am a fantastic supervisor. I bark orders at the kids, run surprise inspections ("That lefse is not round or thin enough! Do it again!"), and refresh cocktails as needed. The workers accept my interference because they know what reward lies ahead. Once the final ball is flattened and cooked, it is my turn to enter the kitchen and churn out a dozen "lefse pizzas" for our hungry group.

At a lefse gathering a few years ago, my friend Kathryn's mom, Carolyn, joined us for the first time. (Kathryn is the friend that I used to force to roll hot *krumkaka* with her bare fingers.) Carolyn has been making lefse for years, using a lefse stick (for transferring rounds to and from the griddle) that her industrious and practical husband made using an old wooden blind slat. She knows what she's doing.

Carolyn entered the kitchen, took one look at my warm, lumpy dough, and immediately asked, "When did you add the flour to this dough?"

"I added it yesterday, after the cooked potatoes had cooled. It has been chilling ever since."

Carolyn tsk-tsked and shook her head sadly. "You never add the flour until right before you roll the dough."

After more than a decade of lefse making, I still have much to learn. Marrying a Norwegian did not improve my skills. However, it did lead to one of the most precious gifts I've ever received, when my mother-in-law, Maureen, presented me with a lefse rolling pin that has been in her family for over one hundred years. The pin is enormous, about twice the size of rolling pins we use now. In fact, the sleeve we keep around it barely clothes even half of the cylinder. It is one piece of wood, with long ridges hand-carved along the length of the pin, and handles smooth with the wear of time and use. It is a breathtaking treasure, and it works well to give texture to lefse rounds and Swedish thin breads alike. I felt my life had come full circle when my son-in-law was the first to put Maureen's rolling pin to use at our next lefse party.

Lefse pizza is one of those spectacular dishes that a cook can pretend is far more difficult to create than it actually is. In fact, I encourage cooks to mimic the lady in the Rice Krispies commercial with a spattering of flour and an expression of martyrdom. Lefse pizza is simply lefse crisped in the oven, then spread with a thin layer of crème fraîche and topped with herbs, quick-pickled vegetables, and luscious bites of gravlax.

**Crisped lefse** also makes a delicious and unique chip for dipping. Slice lefse into smaller sections, brush with olive oil, and bake as on page 234. Serve with lingonberry salsa, combining equal parts of your favorite salsa (add a squeeze of lime and handful of cilantro if using jarred) with lingonberry preserves.

# Vegan **Lefse**

¼ cup vegan butter product (Smart Balance Butter Spread), melted

4 cups riced potatoes, chilled (see tip)

½ cup unsweetened almond milk

2 teaspoons sugar

1 teaspoon salt

1 ½ cups flour

Add melted butter spread to cold potatoes and stir until just combined; add milk, sugar, and salt and stir until rough dough forms. DO NOT OVERMIX. Chill 2 hours or overnight.

Mix in flour. Form into walnut-sized balls, keeping dough chilled during process: dough will rise when it warms. Use a rolling pin fitted with a sleeve to roll into thin rounds. (Norwegian lore says that a rolled lefse round should be almost translucent, although I've also heard that super-thin lefse is vanity in action.)

Use a long flat stick to transfer lefse to hot griddle. Cook until round begins to bubble up. Carefully fold edge of lefse to check for golden brown spots. Run the stick beneath the lefse and carefully flip the round, cooking it an additional minute or until the bottom side has light brown spots.

**MAKES 12–15 ROUNDS**

  **TIP:** Peel and place whole baking- or roasting-style potatoes in cold unsalted water just to cover. Bring to boil and cook until just tender. Drain potatoes and allow to cool completely. Push through ricer and chill at least 2 hours.

# Gravlax **Pizza**

olive oil

1 large lefse round

⅓ cup crème fraîche

2–3 ounces gravlax, sliced thin or cubed

pickled cucumbers

red onions, sliced thin

capers

caviar

fresh dill

fresh chives

Preheat oven to 325 degrees. Brush a generous amount of olive oil on each side of lefse round. Place on baking sheet and bake about 10 minutes, until just crisp, flipping halfway through, taking care not to burn.

Remove lefse from oven and spread crème fraîche over top. Dot with salmon, cucumbers, onion, capers, caviar, dill, and chives. Cut into pieces and serve immediately.

**1 LEFSE ROUND SERVES 2–4**

I spent one weekend afternoon each year, right before Christmas, stabbing whole cloves into an orange. The task was exciting until it began. My older sisters always had beautiful plans of attack, mapping out their oranges so that the cloves formed breathtaking patterns across each orb.

I watched their patient work and tried to imitate them, but by the time I'd pushed a dozen cloves into the thick skin of my orange, my fingers were raw and threatening to bleed. Once our work was complete, our mom would tie beautiful ribbons around the fruit, and our spicy citrus sachets became gifts for teachers.

# Orange & Clove
## Pomander

1 orange

2 ounces whole cloves (purchase from bulk section)

piercing tool, such as a paper piercer or skinny ice pick

2 (18- to 24-inch) strips cloth ribbon

If you want to make a template, poke your orange with the piercing tool to form a pattern. Insert spiky end of cloves into each hole. If you are a free-former, poke and insert cloves willy-nilly. Cross ribbons at the bottom of orange and wrap, evenly spaced, to top of orange. Tie top of ribbons together and form a bow.

Every year I asked if I could make more than one clove-spiked orange, and my mom would always smile and say, "We'll see." She knew I was barely able to complete one, much less multiple fragrant pomanders: more times than not my sister Susan completed my orange, knowing I hadn't the patience or the stamina to do it myself. I think I was born with the calloused fingers of a writer (in just the right places for repeated contact with pencils and keypads, I told myself with pride); sharp, jagged cloves pierced my tender fingertips.

Yet, how I loved the smell! I could work through the pain while my nose stayed fresh. Oranges and cloves are the scents of Christmas, and their presence signals the season is in full swing.

Modern orange pomanders are popular in America and Europe. My mom remembers making them when she was a child. They are so common in Scandinavia that many incorrectly believe the tradition began there. In fact, it is a practice that has its roots in the Middle Ages, when perfumed sachets were believed to have medicinal powers and were used as protection (and for recovery) from sickness and evil.

# Christmas
## IN JULY
## & THE THREE
## WISE WOMEN

Temps soared into the nineties and the humidity was close behind. My husband at the helm of our little car, we sped along the highway, passing semis loaded with lumber and a few wide-loads transporting giant deconstructed wind turbines. I was the designated map gal, using my finger to connect the dots from the Twin Cities to Mahtowa. Mahtowa is one of those little towns that old-timers and up-north people know but that neither of us had heard of before, let along visited.

About an hour outside of the suburbs, we lost my favorite radio station and passed the next two hours listening to podcasts and admiring the corn and soy growing on either side of the highway. Minnesotans use the term "God's Country" when we explore the farms and forests that span our state. We even use the phase occasionally when we venture into neighboring states, but we don't admit that to non-Minnesotans.

It was July. Too hot to imagine Christmas; the air too heavy for meatballs and cream gravy, too sunny and green to crave cookies or bake bread, too sticky to imagine lutfisk fresh from the oven. We navigated through small towns that became smaller with each mile north, until eventually we found our way to a pristine lake on the edge of Mahtowa.

My hostess, Susan, had contacted me earlier in the summer and sent a package that contained examples of her Scandinavia-influenced artwork and books, including colorful images of Dala horses frolicking with costumed Swedes, *tomte*, and *julbockar* (Christmas bucks, that is, Christmas goats), and a children's book based on Susan's own experience eating lutfisk as a child. Susan also sent me some of her favorite Christmas recipes and invited me to Mahtowa to meet with her

and two friends so we could chat about their Christmas traditions. She wrote of her favorite recipes:

> [Rye bread and meatballs] are the two ALWAYS on our *Jul* [table], whether spent with our daughter and family or here. When here we get together with two siblings' families, and these are my contribution musts for our *smörgåsbord*.

> When our daughter was little and before she married, we always had a formal *jul* dinner/*smörgåsbord* of meatballs, ham, *potatis korv* [potato sausage], boiled potatoes, milk rice (with one almond), *fruktsoppa* [fruit soup], *knäckabröd*, rye bread, butter, and assorted cookies for dessert: spritz (not as perfectly shaped as my grandmother's!), rosettes, and our frosted cutout sugar cookies. I always made Swedish coffee rings, for us and to use as gifts.

Along the gravel road to Susan's lake are homes rich with her family history. Susan's cottage, built by her grandfather and an uncle, is next to a stone cabin also built by her grandfather. Each tree and every rock has a story entwined with Susan's heritage. In fact, the entire area is wrapped with the voices of Susan's family. Her grandfather's book, *History of Mahtowa*, is still sold at local stores.

I purposely set our meeting after 1 PM so Susan wouldn't feel obligated to serve a meal, but on the deck overlooking the lake was a beautifully set table with an impressive platter of *smörgåsar* (open-faced turkey and ham sandwiches, vibrant with every fresh and colorful vegetable imaginable concealing the rye bread beneath the toppings as if an accomplished Danish chef had prepared them). It was obvious that Susan was not the kind of person to invite guests and not feed them.

Susan's friends and neighbors Rachel and Cynthia joined us and immediately began telling their stories. They had the energy of three puppies and played off one another as good friends do, always including me in on the joke. They were the Three Wise Women, exchanging banter about politics, religion, and education; life in small towns; and the history of their piece of Mahtowa. They rejoiced in their friendship, in

their agreements and disagreements. They listened carefully when another spoke of her Christmas traditions, asking questions about the unfamiliar and nodding heads at the familiar, such as salt being the spice of choice in their homes. "Only salt, no pepper," Rachel admitted. "To this day I have salt in my pepper shakers."

The Swedish American community is a relatively small one. We soon learned that we had friends and colleagues in common. "When you see Bruce, you tell him I said 'Hello!'" And when the women heard I was interviewing former Minnesota governor Arne Carlson, they laughed and one chimed, "You tell that Arne Carlson he is the only Republican I ever voted for."

Susan was raised in Lindsborg, Kansas, and her Mahtowa grandparents drove down to Kansas for every holiday. In fact, they came a week ahead of Christmas to make sure the lutfisk was properly soaked. "They had to drive rather than fly, so they could bring all of the cookies," Susan said, referring to the dozens of Christmas cookies her grandmother baked. Grandma Lilly Anderson's cookies were legendary. Lilly also prepared *dopp i gryta*, a roast with plenty of au jus to dip rye bread into.

On Christmas Eve the family dressed up, played Swedish and Norwegian hymns, and "Grandma toe-tapped all day while she cooked." This was also when the tree was decorated while the family sang "*Jul Egen*" (Jul Again). Susan recalled annual *smörgåsbord* gatherings: "I remember meatballs and cookies, and being told not to take more than one cookie."

After lunch, the four of us drove a few miles to Rachel's place. The cottage reminded me of summer homes my Swedish friends tell me about. No running water, but heat for the winter, and decorated with musical instruments, paintings, and Scandinavian mementos. Rachel made a pot of egg coffee, using eggs from the chickens that mingle with her cat and her brother's dog in the gardens that sprawl throughout her land. The coffee was smooth, reminding me of fond afternoons spent with my favorite auntie.

Someone brought out homemade strawberry ice cream and cookies, and Rachel gave me her Swedish son-in-law's recipe for *Flygande Jakob*. Flying Jacob is what I like to describe as Swedish hot dish, without the canned soup. Typically, it is layers of chicken, Italian seasoning, bananas, and cream whipped with chili sauce, served over rice and topped with bacon and peanuts. Rachel told me her son-in-law makes his with pineapple rather than banana. She included a business card for her son-in-law and daughter's Swedish gift shop in Stillwater, Minnesota. "Give him a call! He can give you all sorts of great recipes!"

As our conversation returned to Christmas, it included descriptions of modern lutfisk and meatball feeds that the three friends attend together each winter; they talked over one another about which community center or church has the best. Cynthia confessed, "One year I did three of those dinners, and I said, 'Two is enough.'" We all laughed at her assertion.

Susan added, "I associate that smell, opening up the foil and smelling the lutfisk, with Christmas. Now it is Christmas."

# Egg *Kaffe*

**Rachel M. Johnson, Mahtowa, Minnesota**

Include the eggshells if you like, to decrease acidity.

2 tablespoons coffee grounds

1 egg for up to 8 cups water

1 cup cold water

Mix coffee grounds and egg with a fork. Dump into kettle or pot of water. Heat but do not boil. Strain; serve.

SERVES 1

# We all have a memory

of what Christmas sounds like, smells like, tastes like, feels like. For me, it is meatballs frying in butter, herring and gravlax teetering dangerously on thin slices of *knäckbröd*, ginger cookies baking in the oven, citrus poked with cloves, cinnamon and anise floating in a pot of hot wine, and creamy macaroni and cheese topped with crispy, buttery bread crumbs. December 13 wouldn't be the same without warm saffron buns shaped like a pig's tail. The lead-up to the big day wouldn't be as celebratory if I didn't sit in a church basement passing the allspice and arguing with good-hearted strangers about whether or not lefse should be sugared (it shouldn't). Christmas morning wouldn't be Christmas without my mom's almond Danish.

I think often of my great-auntie Hazel and how we created our own Christmas celebration that didn't include anything Swedish outside of our heritage. Our first year celebrating an early Christmas together I asked what I could bring for lunch. Aunt Hazel told me, "I like those McDonald's hamburgers." It became our annual holiday tradition for me to pick up burgers and fries at the drive-through on my way to her place in northeast Minneapolis.

That first year it was just the two of us. She set the table with her Christmas finest, complete with holiday stemware. As I settled in, Aunt Hazel clasped her hands together and asked, "Would you like a glass of wine?" That year I learned that chilled Chablis from a jug pairs perfectly with McDonald's quarter-pounders, and that while she claimed not to speak Swedish, Aunt Hazel could indeed speak the language after a glass (or two) of wine.

All of this is Christmas. All of this reminds me of my Swedish roots and my heartland heritage. Christmas is about embracing the people and flavors that we love. It means serving a dish from the culture of a new family member or putting a unique spin on old recipes; adding lefse, *rømmegrøt*, Asian-style meatballs, and McDonald's fries to the Swedish *julbord*; inviting newcomers to dine with the traditional, and inventing a unique mosaic of cuisine and culture.

Perhaps, like my great-grandmother, you add a hefty hot dish of macaroni and cheese to make your son happy, to welcome your daughter-in-law, and to affirm that you and your family are Americans.

I don't have my great-grandmother's recipe for macaroni and cheese. I don't even know if there ever was a recipe, or if she just threw in a little of this, a little of that, like many of us do. Christmas is magical like that. In the heartland we embrace our heritage, honor those who came before us, and look to the future together.

# Macaroni and Cheese

¼ cup (½ stick) butter

3 tablespoons flour

1 teaspoon dry mustard

1 teaspoon paprika

1 teaspoon salt

1 teaspoon pepper

4 cups milk, at room temperature

1 cup heavy cream,
at room temperature

4–5 cups grated cheese (use your favorite; any variety will do)

1 pound elbow macaroni,
cooked and drained

1 cup dried bread crumbs mixed
with 1 tablespoon butter

Preheat oven to 350 degrees and grease a large (3-quart) casserole dish. Melt butter in large pot; add flour and seasonings and whisk about 3 to 5 minutes. Slowly add stream of milk to roux, whisking all the while. Bring to simmer, continuing to whisk, about 2 minutes. Roux should thicken. Add cream and handfuls of cheese and stir until melted. Combine cheese sauce with macaroni. Transfer mixture to prepared dish. Sprinkle buttered bread crumbs evenly over casserole. Bake for 30 to 40 minutes or until topping browns and bubbles.

**SERVES 12**

# acknowledgments

Every writer I know has prepared the acknowledgements for her first book well before she ever had a topic, a publisher, or an editor. Like the speech you write in case you win an Oscar, every writer I know forgets to name someone important when pen finally hits paper. At the risk of forgetting someone I should be thanking, I begin by simply thanking everyone I've ever met, spoken to, smiled at, laughed and cried with, or sat next to on the bus. I also want to thank everyone I've ever read, admired, watched on TV, or listened to on the radio. You know who you are. Thank you to the chefs, home cooks, and food writers who constantly inspire me, feed me, thrill me. A special shout-out to every dog I've ever petted, every cat whose internet video made me smile (that includes you, Keyboard Cat), and every slice of warm buttered bread ever delivered to my mouth.

Now that that's out of the way . . .

I owe much gratitude to the Minnesota Historical Society Press and the American Swedish Institute for agreeing to guide me on this edible journey. Thanks to my ridiculously amazing editor (with the ridiculously cool editor's name), Shannon Pennefeather, for propping me up, coddling my fragile ego, and finding the right words when I couldn't. Thanks also to designer Susan Everson for making things prettier (and the superb fonts), and to publishing coach Scott Edelstein for nodding calmly when I get all excited about pickled herring.

Thank you to the University of Minnesota's College of Continuing Education, and the faculty, staff, and students from the (sadly now defunct) Master's of Liberal Studies, where the seeds of this query were planted. Thanks also to Roger Miller for insisting that I take Swedish language classes, meet some nice church basement bakers, and write with enthusiasm.

A special thanks to my coworkers who ate more fried rosettes, buttered *tunnbröd*, and rice puddings than they probably want to admit. Tiffany and John, your sausage-making expertise saved me! And Kathryn, my partner in eating epiphanies, we'll always have Aquavit Minneapolis, the ABBA Museum, and meals that cost more than my mortgage.

Mom, you taught your five daughters how to converse at the dinner table. You created a loud, eager, opinionated crew, and when one of us is missing at the table we are incomplete. My stories were never as entertaining as those told by my four older, wiser, dazzling sisters, but because of that I learned to write. You also taught us to laugh loudly, smile at strangers, and embrace our curiosity. Thank you for giving me my sisters; without them I'd be storyless, and without them I'd have no one to fill in the blanks when my memory muddies. Thank you for embracing Dad's Swedish traditions, even though they were not your own, and giving them to us.

Dad, thanks for showing us that there is nothing wrong with burned meatballs, and for loving me in the ways you knew how. That is always enough.

A final, rousing thanks goes to the individuals who so generously shared their time, stories, food traditions, recipes, and endless cups of good coffee. Your contributions are a living heritage.

# for further reading

Brown, Dale. *The Cooking of Scandinavia*. New
York: Time-Life Books, Time, Inc., 1968.

Brown, Linda Keller, and Kay Mussell, eds. *Ethnic and Regional
Foodways in the United States: The Performance of Group
Identity*. Knoxville: University of Tennessee Press, 1984.

Carheden, Görel Kristina. *Food and Festivals: Swedish
Style*. Minneapolis: Dillon Press, 1968.

Dooley, Beth, and Lucia Watson. *Savoring the Seasons of the
Northern Heartland*. New York: Alfred A. Knopf, 1994.

Gordon, Milton M. *Assimilation in American Life: The Role of Race, Religion,
and National Origins*. New York: Oxford University Press, 1964.

Kalcik, Susan. "Ethnic Foodways in America." In Brown
and Mussell, *Ethnic and Regional Foodways*.

Kaplan, Anne, Marjorie A. Hoover, and Willard B. Moore. *The Minnesota
Ethnic Food Book*. St. Paul: Minnesota Historical Society Press, 1986.

Kaplan, Anne R., Marjorie A. Hoover, and Willard B. Moore. "On Ethnic
Foodways." In Shortridge and Shortridge, eds., *The Taste of American Place*.

Kurlansky, Mark, ed. *The Food of a Younger Land: A Portrait of American
Food: Before the National Highway System, Before Chain Restaurants, and
Before Frozen Food, When the Nation's Food was Seasonal, Regional, and
Traditional: From the Lost WPA Files*. New York: Riverhead Books, 2009.

Lanegran, David. "Swedes in the Twin Cities." American Swedish
Institute Forum lecture series, Minneapolis, January 28, 2009.

MacClancy, Jeremy. *Consuming Culture: Why You Are What
You Eat*. New York: Henry Holt and Company, 1992.

Rice, John G. "The Swedes." In *They Chose Minnesota: A
Survey of the State's Ethnic Groups*, edited by June Drenning
Holmquist. St. Paul: Minnesota Historical Society Press, 1981.

Shortridge, Barbara G., and James R. Shortridge, eds. *The Taste of American Place:
A Reader on Regional and Ethnic Foods*. Lanham, MD: Rowman & Littlefield, 1998.

Thursby, Jacqueline. *Foodways and Folklore: A Handbook*.
Westport, CT: Greenwood Press, 2008.

# recipe index

From top: Orange Almond Melting Moments (page 61), Spritz (page 72), and *Pepparkakor* (pages 63–64)

*Pulla*, for Cardamom Toast Ice Cream with Lingonberry Jam (page 218)

# SUBJECT INDEX

Katie Schaumann

# About the Author

Patrice Johnson is a Nordic food geek and meatball historian. She writes food and culture posts for a variety of web and print publications as well as the weekly column "Called to the Table" for the *Gaylord Hub* (Sibley County, Minnesota). She teaches Nordic food classes and presents interactive cooking demonstrations at sites throughout the Twin Cities and beyond.

*Jul* was designed and set in type by
Susan Everson in St. Paul, Minnesota.
The typefaces are Storyteller and
Quasimoda. The book was printed
by Friesens, Altona, Canada.